MARKETING COMMUNICATIONS FOR SOLICITORS

A practical guide to promoting your firm

by Mark Oglesby BA (Hons)
Consultant to Trowers & Hamlins, Solicitors

First published in Great Britain 1994 by Cavendish Publishing Limited, The Glass House, Wharton Street, London WC1X 9PX

Telephone: 071-278 8000 Facsimile: 071-278 8080

© Oglesby, M 1994

All rights reserved. No part of this publication may be reproduced or transmitted in any form or by any means, electronic or mechanical, photocopying, recording or otherwise, without the prior permission of the publisher and copyright owner.

The right of the author of this work has been asserted in accordance with the Copyright, Designs and Patents Act 1988.

Any person who infringes the above in relation to this publication may be liable to criminal prosecution and civil claims for damages.

British Library Cataloguing in Publication Data

Oglesby, Mark
Marketing Communications for Solicitors
I Title
344.200688

ISBN 1-874241-19-8
Printed and bound in Great Britain

dedicated to my wife Nicol
with love

Preface

This book outlines practical steps in promoting a firm of solicitors – and by extension, most forms of partnership. It is not a handbook on marketing.

Since the author cannot claim expertise in strategic issues, he has abjured – happily – the right to add to the existing body of literature on such matters as pricing, product/service evolution, distribution of services or general theoretical guidance.

Promoting Professional Practices aims to provide marketing executives, partners and fee earners with helpful advice on conducting promotional activities. It takes its premise from the impression that, with more than enough theory in professional services firms (both workable and impractical), there is a dearth of advice on 'how to do it'.

Because it is written for the lawyer as well as the marketing professional, the book assumes no knowledge from the reader of marketing, public relations, promotional media, or their jargon.

Promoting Professional Practices presupposes that a firm's business plan, policy and objectives already exist, or are being addressed by marketing strategists. However, for any firm Luddite enough to believe it can do without planned marketing – but which is nevertheless willing to consider some new-fangled techniques to drum up business – this book may help ensure that the promotional structure serves a purpose. Even if the foundations are absent.

In most of the areas covered by the text, there is no such thing as a defined, correct approach. Opinions expressed are just that - opinions. However, they arise from the author's experience, buttressed or tempered by the views of a cross-section of colleagues within the professional services field.

It is customary, at this point in an introduction, to offer a disclaimer along the lines of 'the credit for factual information belongs to innumerable colleagues, friends and selfless contributors; the errors are all mine'. Since early marketing and promotion of law firms has been characterised by recurrent reinvention of square wheels, and since I must have learned something from such a process, it would be arrogant of me to lay claim to all errors in this book.

However, I do beg the reader's pardon for any horrors of factual inaccuracy undetected by me, and his or her forbearance when it comes to perceived errors of interpretation. If any take violent objection to guidance given, I (along with Cromwell) 'beseech you, in the bowels of Christ, think it possible you may be mistaken'.

The structuring and integration of marketing disciplines into law firms is, in the main, only now being addressed correctly. Thus the rules relating to the subject of this book remain loose. This enables any fool to write any foolishness, without fear of being unmasked. I trust that I have not abused the freedom this lends by producing observations without foundation or guidance without objectivity.

As for those who have helped me produce this book, my primary debt is to the Partners of Trowers & Hamlins.

Particular thanks is owed to Don Moorhouse, the firm's managing partner, and partner Jennie Gubbins, who were kind enough not only to authorise the sharing of my experience, gained through serving the firm, but also to read draft copy. A third partner of the firm, David Mosey, also took the time and trouble to comment on the draft text. The critiques of all three were constructive and helped shape the final version.

Stephen Clues of Trowers & Hamlins was equally generous with his time in reading draft copy; as head of business development he was able to add a marketing perspective, pertinent comment and advice, for which he has my gratitude. As does Clare Usher, who has imposed discipline and efficiency on me in her role as my assistant over the past four years. I would also mention Nick White, Neil Cohen and Ian Graham, partners whose long-term support of promotional initiatives within the firm has brought with it a level of personal support which has made working with them a pleasure.

In discussions with colleagues and fellows within the legal market, many have proved helpful, others less so. Falling clearly within the former category, I owe a particular debt of gratitude to marketing consultant Kim Tasso and Lynn Hill of Taylor Joynson Garrett, both of whom made free not only with their time and opinions, but also furnished me with copies of their previously published views on areas germane to this book.

Thanks are also owed and given with appreciation to Georgina Schneeman, Martyn Gowar, Sarah Dean and Matthew Fuller, all of whom were prepared to share their experiences gratis. While some of their words have found their way into print, I can only hope that they will forgive the mass of useful observations plagiarised or subsumed into my own text.

Peter Bushell, a fine designer, and Mark Turner, a conscientious printer, have helped me enormously over the years; their contributions to this book are hidden but substantial. The same acknowledgement of past and present support applies to Mike Mansfield, who has allowed me unrestricted access to his PR knowledge for a decade. I am also grateful to Peter Belsey of Huthwaite, and Cristina Stuart of SpeakEasy Training Ltd, for their specialist advice on Sales and Presentation techniques respectively.

For permission to quote from the Solicitors Publicity Code, and their advice on matters of interpretation, I thank the Law Society – and Susannah Lewis of the Professional Ethics Division in particular.

Finally, I offer a debt of gratitude and a howl of anguish to Jo Reddy, who commissioned this book. Only now do I understand the pride of the writer and the true horror of the writing.

Table of contents

Preface i

1 The background to marketing communications 1
The PR man cometh 1
Public relations 2
The PR coup 3
Promoting a firm 4
The marketing context 6
Why promote? 6
Recent change: the industrial parallel 8
The advent of promotion 9
The current situation 10
No choice but to market 11
The advent of effective planning 12
The culture gap 13
A perfect world (a marketing fantasy) 14
The implication for promotional work 15
Running in-house promotional services 22

2 Corporate identity 23
The corporate identity brief 29
Summary 31
Hints and tips 34

3 Advertising 35
Lawyers' advertising to date 35
Why should you advertise? 35
Basic guidelines 36
Should you advertise against a special feature, or in isolation? . .37
What to say 38
Think client 42
Response mechanism 42
Reinforcement 42
Factual or creative? Regular or occasional? 43
General guidelines 43
Professional help 45
Start with a designer 45

v

Steps along the way 47
Selectivity 48
In short 53
Summary 53
Hints and tips 55

4 Media relations 57
1. 'It's who you know, not what you know' 57
2. 'All publicity is good publicity' 58
3. 'Most journalists are only interested in hatchet jobs' 58
A truth 59
The importance of journalists 60
What to do when contacted by the media 60
Summary 76
Hints and tips 78

5 Publications 81
What is a publication? 81
Form and content 82
The publications range 82
Publication essentials 83
What does it cost? 84
Getting started on a corporate brochure 85
Write a brief 85
The limits of consultation 87
Drafting 87
What size should it be? 91
Newsletters 91
Information vehicles 92
Photography and illustrations 92
Design and print 93
From concept to publication 95
Do it yourself 95
Typesetters 96
Choosing your typeface 97
Jargon 97
Colour 98
Proofs and the printing process 99
Going to print 100
Other printing options 100
Choosing your paper stock 101

Binding	101
The print run	102
Run ons	103
Summary	104
Hints and tips	105

6 Speaking in public 107

Tailor to time	108
Think from the audience's point of view – not your own	108
Sell yourself – not your subject	108
Keep it simple	110
Tell or sell?	110
Getting started	110
Paint pictures; inject life	111
Break down the divide	112
Format, not content	113
Audience attention spans	113
Preparation and practice	114
Giving the speech	115
Visual aids	116
Your demeanour and appearance	117
Body language	118
Ending well	119
Questions	119
Documentation	120
In smaller gatherings	121
Summary	123
Hints and tips	124

7 Beauty parades and proposal documents 125

The proposal document	125
Packaging and delivery	127
The brief	128
Research	128
Establishing rapport	129
Keep it simple	129
Timing and length	130
Patience and practice	131
Be human!	131
Summary	133
Hints and tips	133

vii

8 Crisis management 135
What is a crisis? 135
Preparing people 136
Statements and no comment 136
Responding to calls 138
Taking the initiative 138
Other enquiries 140
The silver lining 140
The crisis management exercise 141
Summary 143

9 Corporate hospitality and sponsorship 145
The rationale 145
The approach 146
The sponsorship route 147
Exploitation 148
Building community relations 148
What can be sponsored? 149
Other subjects 150
Sponsorship agencies 150
Summary 151
Checklist: to what are you entitled? 151

10 Database 153
Marketing records 156
Objections 157
How to choose a database 159
Summary 161

11 Exhibitions 163
What is the point of exhibiting? 163
How to choose the right exhibition 164
Location 165
Shell scheme – or space only? 166
Bespoke stands 166
Promotional literature 167
Differentiate yourself 167
Preparing for an exhibition 168
Exhibition techniques 168
Record keeping 170
Follow up 171
Checklist of administrative stand arrangements 173

viii

Summary	174
Hints and tips	175

12 Seminars 177

When to hold a seminar	178
Planning	178
Partner involvement	179
Who should speak?	179
Who should be invited?	180
Choice of venue	181
Timetable and administration	183
Letter of invitation	184
Coordinator	184
Follow up mailings	185
Meetings	185
Internal support	185
Badging	185
How many will turn up?	186
Preparation and presentation of material	186
Preparing and giving presentations	188
Checklist: holding an event	190
Summary	193
Hints and tips	194

13 Research 195

The alternative to research	195
What you already know	196
What can be researched?	196
The case for, and the case against	198
When to research	199
Setting the brief	199
Who should do the work?	200
Presenting research	201
Summary	202
Hints and tips	202

14 Direct mail 203

What is direct mail?	203
A case history	204
The obvious option	205
What form should it take?	205

Who to mail 206
Summary 207
Hints and tips 207

15 Continuous promotion 209
Establishing a norm 210
Content 210
Enthusiasm 211
Social promotion 212
Research yourself 213
Associations 213
Keeping in touch 214
Summary 215
Hints and tips 215

Appendix I 217
Solicitors' Publicity Code 1990
(with consolidated amendments to 1 January 1992) 217
Appendix II 221
Selected Bibliography 221
Appendix III 223
A selection of addresses and contacts 223

x

1 The background to marketing communications

Terminology is where it began to go wrong.

When lawyers first had to face the spectre of marketing, the word carried a variety of unpleasant connotations: selling, more work – even crassness. The profession sorely needed advisors who could communicate clearly what marketing entailed and how it could play its part in a legal practice.

Unfortunately, that is not what it got.

Those few who found themselves faced by the real McCoy – an accurate definition of marketing – found the conceptual leap too great to handle. The true marketeers failed to recognise how alien was the concept they were trying to communicate. The lawyers recoiled.

What appeared to be on offer belied the comforting and established order of things. It looked at long-term planning without short-term gain. Practices were transformed into businesses, selling to customers. The marketeers promised nothing and produced paper.

Such a lack of instant results was judged against a time of plenty. Jam tomorrow is a difficult concept when one is already enjoying a fair amount of jam today.

The PR man cometh

With a sigh of relief, the lawyers welcomed the public relations professionals. White knight consultancies rode in, promising that they would produce the business plans, the marketing strategies et al, but that they would also drum up acres of media coverage, take on discreet yet effective advertising, conduct research, draw together a corporate identity, run exhibitions and seminars and, in short, act as a one stop shop for all possible marketing functions and consultancy.

Unfortunately, someone was being deluded. The lawyers. PR people tend to know a lot about PR and very little about marketing. Since lawyers knew little about either, PR people were able to claim expertise that they rarely had. Suddenly, they were marketing supremos.

In the Autumn of 1991, Robert Pay, head of marketing at Clifford Chance, was quoted in *Business Marketing Review,* defining the head of marketing in law firms as 'an ex PR person, or an ex lawyer, or an ex journalist, most of whom are struggling with marketing concepts generally, let alone the slightly more sophisticated ones you need for professional services'.

So on one side were the amateur marketeers, out of their depth. On the other were the academics, who walked on water. Most had no idea of how to direct law firms towards practical navigation.

Roger Bruce, head of business development at Herbert Smith, refers to 'a wing of serious academic marketeers specialising in thorough analysis of data and the pursuance of marketing philosophies and a wing of "entrepreneurial types" with their main focus on promotion and PR ... on the one hand you have data overload and on the other it's all fuzz'.

With the benefit of hindsight, most partners now involved in the marketing of their firm would be able to ask a few pertinent questions, receive a few impertinent replies, and then send the PR consultant (journalist or lawyer manqué) packing.

Public relations

PR is a nebulous term at the best of times. At its most limited, it is confused with press relations. To a PR consultant and most clients, it means public relations. PR used correctly suffuses every element of a firm's behaviour. In *Public Relations Techniques,* Frank Jefkins describes PR as 'the ears as well as the voice of an organisation.' Thus, because communication is common to all aspects of all organisations, PR has a universal part to play.

Thus the difference between press – simply liaising between journalist and client – and public, in this context, is enormous. The public is everything and everyone.

To control the communication process, PR selects appropriate 'publics' and aims to manage a client's reputation in relation to these groups. Thus public relations consultants aim to look after any form of communication between a client organisation and those with whom it has valued contact.

A LAW FIRM'S PUBLICS

Fig 1

PR sets out to achieve 'mutual understanding' with these 'publics'. It is a communication business. As such, it plays a vital role across a firm, but also within the marketing function, as part of the marketing approach. At its most nebulous (ie in shaping a firm's image), it can be claimed that PR is an independent discipline. On the promotional side, however, it cannot operate properly until the marketing strategy has been established.

PR follows, develops and enacts. As law firms found, it should not lead.

The PR coup

When lawyers looked to exploit new freedoms in self-promotion, PR appropriated all the available territory. While it could rightly claim that it could look after most promotional work ('marketing communications') that lawyers might contemplate, it did great damage by claiming to be a synonym for marketing.

As Kim Tasso observed as early as 1991, 'Many of the law firms that appear to have embraced marketing principles have really just embraced the practice of marketing communications. Sadly, the plethora of glossy brochures, newsletters, press releases, mailshots, seminars and advertisements demonstrates that the majority of practitioners see marketing as a superficial "optional extra" without the solid foundations of business plans, marketing strategies, product development and market research.'

The legacy is that many partners in UK law firms cannot now differentiate between marketing and public relations.

Promoting a firm

And now here I am talking about 'promoting' a law firm. What does that mean?

Promotion is defined here as any activity designed to communicate the lawyer's offer to the world. It is part of the marketing process. Thus it is also referred to as marketing communication.

Marketing shapes and manages a firm's offer. Promotion is the aspect of marketing which allows that message to be communicated. PR – the management of reputation – is thus both a constant and intangible part of the promotional aspect of marketing. Far from being a synonym for the entire process, it is but a contributor when it comes to practical marketing initiatives.

Figure 2 may help clarify the distinction, showing how marketing provides the foundations on which promotional activities are built and which dictate their shape.

Note: In order to prevent over-scrupulous specifications from obscuring this text's readability, I will refer to 'marketeers' as a catch-all grouping, when looking at general communication subject matter. Thus this term embraces marketing strategists, PR people, promotional experts, general consultants and in-house specialists.

Fig 2

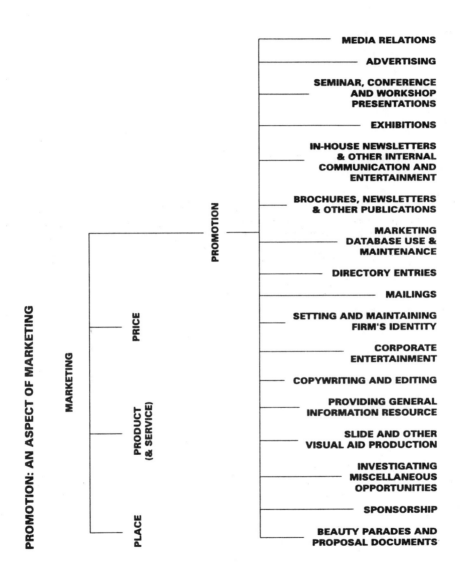

The marketing context

Having seen how PR and marketing became intertwined, let us look at the equally inauspicious attempts to put matters right.

In the late 1980s, substantial investment was made by forms of solicitors, particularly the larger ones, in recruiting experienced marketing professionals. The results were decidedly mixed. Despite previous records of success, some marketeers were unable to adapt to the style of their respective firms; equally, many firms failed to match the talents of the personnel with the job for which they had been selected. Indeed, senior strategic marketing professionals often found themselves doing a pure marketing communications job – writing brochures, organising seminars and being kept at arm's length from the partnership.

Many firms now accept marketing under this incomplete definition, leaving it divorced from influence over which markets should be served and which services are offered. However, as Stephen Clues of Trowers & Hamlins points out, 'the more for-sighted firms are reaching a situation in which the role of marketing includes targeting and target setting, market-planning, skills transfer, training and other established marketing disciplines'. As in his own case (he is Head of Business Development) there is a trend towards describing marketing jobs filled by marketing people in non-marketing terms.

The challenge for these more progressive firms is to stand four-square behind a consensus on their marketing plans and to match their staff allocation and recruitment, and all resources, to the goals agreed.

Why promote?

Somewhere in the above you may have gained a clearer idea of what is meant by marketing and what is meant by promotion. But why is it an issue? Why should anyone promote a law firm or professional practice?

Every firm has an offer, which may be produced almost incidentally, or which marketing sets out to evolve and manage. As the chapter on corporate identity makes clear, every firm has a reputation and an image, whether it works at it or not. In a competitive market, one cannot afford to take a laissez faire attitude. Expertise and features have to be conveyed as benefits to clients. Thus communication is vital.

Out of this context has arisen an enormously important shift in perspective for the legal profession – thinking from the client's point of view.

Speaking many years ago at an ICAS annual conference, customer care guru Dr John Nicholson warned accountants that 'the profession needs to shift from thinking that the accountant knows best to understanding the customer's needs.' It is this shift that lawyers have also had to undergo.

An ICL Legal Survey, conducted among lawyers in July 1991, indicated that 91% of respondents accepted that the public's perception of lawyers was a problem. Despite this high acceptance figure, there was still a huge perception gap between how lawyers saw their offer to clients, and how clients saw what was on offer.

Figure 3, taken from a different survey conducted in the same year, demonstrates this point.

THE PERCEPTION GAP: Quality of Law Firms' Service as seen by Solicitors and the Public

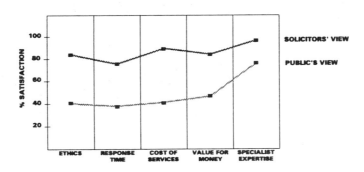

Fig 3   BVA Survey 1991

Such a discrepancy has led, quite rightly, to an understanding that client satisfaction is of primary importance to the legal profession. The firms that will dominate the 1990s will be those that measure their success by 'directly, systematically and routinely measuring client satisfaction', according to Neil Morgan (*Law Notes* June 1992), who goes on to point out that 'the biggest source of client dissatisfaction in the UK is inadequate, late and poor quality client communications'.

While client satisfaction imbues all aspects of marketing, promotional work can be an active and logical response to the need to communicate better. Alternatively, it can perpetuate past failings. The differentiator is whether communication considers first what the client wants to know, or what the lawyer wants to say.

Recent change: the industrial parallel

In coming to view transactions from the client viewpoint, law firms are undergoing a sea change. In some ways, though, their changes are easier to ride than the shifts experienced by industrial concerns, from which lessons have been learned.

Like industry, law was originally production driven. When factories could produce huge amounts of cheap goods, they flourished because there was a natural demand. Equally, without competition, it is arguable that many law firms simply waited for their skills to attract custom.

When industry came to face a slowing market and competition, concerns reacted by learning to sell. The third stage of evolution was then to move from selling to marketing, ie from off-loading to customising in line with a requirement.

Law firms have largely skipped the interim stage. No longer production-driven, some could be said to be moving towards becoming marketing-driven organisations.

THE STRUCTURE OF A MARKETING-BASED FIRM

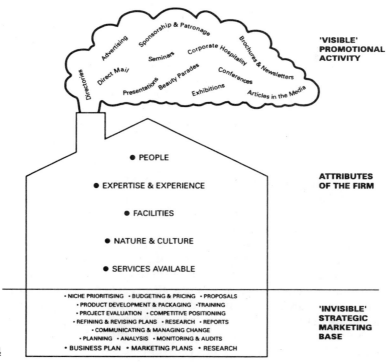

Fig 4

The advent of promotion

So, against this lightly sketched background, we should look at the events which led to such changes, and which eroded the centuries-old prohibition against promotion.

In October 1984 the Law Society followed the precedent set by US lawyers (1977) and UK accountants (1981) by allowing UK law firms to promote their practices.

It was not exactly an opening of the floodgates. As SC Silkin QC observed shortly after, 'the agony which the leaders of the professions suffered in making that leap can be measured by the restrictiveness with which the new licence was promulgated.'

On 1 October 1990, regulations were further relaxed, enabling firms to name clients (with permission) and claim specialisation. Subsequent years have brought further minor liberalisation (more detail on the Law Society Publicity Code can be found in Appendix 1).

Within a few years, the cosy world of the lawyer was under threat. Apparently monstrous new words and phrases entered the legal lexicon, such as 'beauty parade', 'business plan', 'marketing professional', with 'niches' and 'segmentation' rearing ugly heads. A legal article in the *Independent* on 3 April 1992 carried a headline which would have bemused – even appalled – lawyers only a few years before. It claimed that 'It's Not Unprofessional to Sell'.

Law firms had spent centuries defining and developing a highly distinctive culture, in which work was inherited, won through word of mouth or social contacts. Dignity, decency and decorum were of premium importance. These were defined through strictures against improper behaviour. Suddenly, certain aspects once considered improper became acceptable. Small wonder then that what the 1980s considered normal the majority within the legal profession saw as, at best, a necessary evil, born of the times.

Reaction to change was predictable. Many law firms circumnavigated the uncharted waters. A few hailed friendly PR pilots to guide them onto the reefs. Others dropped anchor with their marketing consultants. The majority sailed gingerly close to shore, wearing expressions of distaste before retreating back into harbour. Only one or two hoisted sail and sought to make the most of their opportunities.

So what were the practical problems to be faced?

The answer then is just as valid today. No one knew quite where they were, where they were going, or how to get there. This is still true of the majority of law firms, even today. Some have the vision, but few have put into effect practical marketing plans to get themselves there.

'There's a lot of where we'd like to be and not enough of where we are', explains Martyn Gowar, marketing partner at Lawrence Graham.

THE ROLE OF OPERATIONAL MARKETING (PROMOTION)

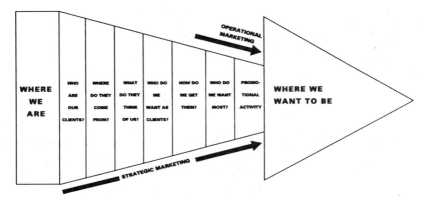

Fig 5

The fact is that firms can be loose agglomerations of fee earners, each of whom jealously guards a client base and works semi-autonomously. That makes self-knowledge hard to come by.

Thus, when looking at where a firm is, the most important questions which arise include: 'Where do we want to get to?' and 'Who are our clients?'

Marketeers will then ask annoying questions such as:

- Are clients being offered what they want – or merely what we want to offer?
- Is the price right?
- What are our competitors doing?

All of these are questions for the partnership and the marketeer. Only when it gets to 'How do we reach these people?' do the marketing communications people come into play.

The current situation

The overall challenge facing the professions is how to maintain profitability in an increasingly competitive marketplace. Addressing this problem requires the establishment of the correct marketing support structure.

By 1994, the PR consultants-as-marketeers have long gone. Those who remain do what they have always been supposed to do – PR. Professional marketeers are now seen as the logical first point of contact. This is as it should be, provided that the marketing consultant or employee has learned the lessons of the 1980s and offers pragmatism as well as academic guidance.

As we have seen however, the way things have evolved, have not been easy for either the marketing professional or the lawyer.

Research carried out in 1992 by Strategic Marketing Consultants showed a lamentably short lifespan for marketing professionals in the legal field. Few could see a long term career ahead of them and many partners saw marketing as a quick fix technique, with the fixer being jettisoned once the work had been completed.

Let us dwell, though, on what has worked. The main change has been one of perception. Firms are now prepared to think of themselves as businesses seeking to meet the needs of their clients. Far fewer presentations or brochures are written by lawyers apparently for fellow lawyers. Client satisfaction surveys are just one manifestation of the change from 'we need to tell them how good we are' to 'we need to find out what they want'.

A realisation has set in that most new work derives from existing clients (the figure of 80% is often quoted). Integrated accounting and marketing databases which record and monitor details of these existing clients are seen as more important than mailing lists of potential contacts.

Practice has improved the standards of seminars and exhibition presence. An understanding has developed, usually in principle, sometimes in fact, of how to use advertising and media relations. Trial and error has overcome the relentless rush of directory entry opportunities. Corporate identity reviews now feature IT facilities and internal documentation, not just the firm's letterhead.

No choice but to market

Perhaps most importantly, most firms now know that they must market. They know this because they have realised that they have always marketed themselves. The Law Society's relaxation of the rules did not introduce a new world, merely new areas to explore. The effectiveness with which individual firms approach these areas determines the concomitant mix of opportunities and problems.

Failing to explore an option is recognised by most as a disastrous course. Those who try to oppose the tide face Canute's dilemma. Some form of marketing response is required of every firm, even if determined simply as a negative response to competitor initiatives.

Any firm claiming that marketing is not for them, and that they offer a traditional service, has missed the point. They need to market themselves as a traditional service, or they will go the traditional route of those obscured by others' attractions.

The advent of effective planning

Finally, the importance of strategic and project planning is now being widely accepted. Thus, greater knowledge of self (the firm) and the target (clients) is leading to more visible, sustainable and effective marketing. In turn, this means that promotional activities are working within a defined structure, not a vacuum.

In short, route planning is becoming natural to the partnership.

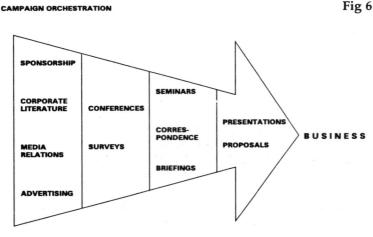

CAMPAIGN ORCHESTRATION   Fig 6

de forte Associates

The culture gap

There is one additional historical hindrance, which perpetuates and must be acknowledged by anyone trying to make progress in the legal marketing field. It could be argued that this factor provided the greatest impediment to professional service promotion in the past.

The problem is people. Or rather, the enormous cultural differences between those from the marketing/PR/promotional side and those from the firm.

Even now, while most firms are resigned to, accept, or welcome marketing and the idea of promoting their practice, there is still an intrinsic gulf between the average lawyer and the average marketeer.

The lawyer is used to control. A watchword is caution. His intelligence is focused on a defined and linear path forward. Detail and total accuracy are pursued in all things. With exceptions, the lawyer is a specialist.

The non-academic marketeer's profile is very different. His world is largely unfettered by precedent, rules or set paths. His areas of interest and expertise are catholic. His approach may be lateral, his options various and his imagination regularly called into play. Again, with exceptions, the marketeer is a jack of many trades.

This is, of course, a simplistic portrait. Many representatives from each camp could lay claim to the other's characteristics. Some qualified lawyers are now full time marketeers. Both jobs require creativity, albeit of a different nature.

Yet for each to communicate easily with the other requires time and patience. The languages spoken are different. The norms, dictates and expectations of the two professions are rarely identical.

Any successful promoter of a law firm or other professional practice needs to grasp this fact. Patience is required to make progress, not an attempt to change the world overnight. Ideas need careful exploration and consideration, not imposition. This is the world of tact, diplomacy and the poker player.

At a Chartered Institute of Marketing lecture some years ago at which those delegates who admitted they were not poker players were invited to leave immediately. The entire lecture proceeded to dwell only on poker hands. Those who have had experience of marketing, and legal marketing in particular, will be able to judge whether there is a relevant lesson here.

The analogy breaks down, of course, on the point of winners and losers. Where poker players calculate, bluff and sneak to success, marketeers need to play a clever team game. If ever 'them and us' becomes thematic, the game is lost.

A recognition that both parties seek the same ends must always be fostered. The alternative, seen all too often in the past, is the frustration that arises when irresistible marketing advice meets immovable legal logic.

The desired result should be a meeting in the middle, where each party has learned to understand – and share – the other's objectives and language. Out of such concord are successfully promoted partnerships born.

A perfect world (a marketing fantasy)

The following presents the unlikely – but not the impossible. If achieved, it would provide the perfect framework for marketing to contribute positively to a law firm's health:

- Strong, respected senior and managing partners, whose views are in harmony.
- Partnership willing to delegate marketing strategy to a marketing committee, 'directed' by a consultant/employee with experience of strategic issues.
- A culture of expectation – partners and fee earners are keen to conduct their own campaigns, promoting themselves, their practice and the firm. They use marketing professionals to advise and guide and promotional resources to support.
- A chargeable hours structure that allows time for practice development.
- Business development research conducted to check assumptions and determine opportunities.
- A business plan, compiled and supported by the marketing committee.
- A marketing plan for the firm, compiled by the marketing consultant/employee.
- A structure for the firm, ideally based not on departments but on client markets. This enables each group within the firm to produce its own specific marketing plan. This is based on advice from the marketing consultant/employee and drawn up with reference to the firm's overall marketing plan.
- Partners prepared to contribute views but accept decisions made by the marketing committee, even if these decisions run contrary to their own views.

- Promotional activities planned well in advance, in order to achieve the objectives of the marketing plans.
- Continuous assessment of the success or failure of promotional and other marketing initiatives. Evolution of the business and marketing plans, to take account of lessons learned.
- A realistic set of expectations (results in mid to long term).
- Up to date and uniform accounting records, on electronic systems.
- Budget readily available for agreed initiatives. Marketing costs seen as an investment, not as an overhead.
- Choice of activities determined primarily through relevance to strategic aims rather than budget.

The implication for promotional work

If the above dream were a reality, then all promotional activities could:

- fall within a logical, explicable and effective structure;
- be planned well in advance;
- work together (more neologistically, they would 'achieve synergy');
- be open to monitoring and assessment;
- be achieved with the minimum of meetings, discussion, contradictory views and disputes.

In this perfect and fertile soil, promotional work has the best chance of flourishing. For it to do so, there are several additional factors which those involved must work or hope for.

Support of senior personnel in the partnership

Unless early agreement can be reached as to the objectives and route necessary to achieve them, then time is wasted. There will be objections from some partners to any initiative that is not hopelessly anodyne; while consultation is important and consensus the objective, decisions are notoriously difficult to reach when determined across a partnership. Therefore, an authoritative decision-making structure will facilitate promotional activity.

Partner commitment

Notwithstanding the above, individual partners need to be won over to the benefits of marketing – and thus promotional activities. Ince &

Co's Director of Marketing Georgina Schneeman talks about persuasion by 'incremental steps', by 'walkabout' and by 'using converts to persuade cynics'. The internal communication process is of absolute importance; without it, there will be a lack of commitment and hence no hope of success.

Additionally, partners must be encouraged by the firm's culture to commit time to promoting their practice. Ideally, they should be accountable for practice development within their sector of the firm, leading to accountability for promotional activity.

Champions

Every initiative needs a champion within the partnership. This is someone who believes strongly in the need to pursue that particular course. The champion also needs to have the weight to carry opinion with him or her.

This relates back to, and is the natural result of, the aforementioned commitment.

There is no point, no matter how marvellous the circumstances, in finding or creating an opportunity and then trying to impose it on a reluctant partnership.

Without active support from a partner, the project will almost certainly fail. Indeed, without partner support, there may even be an unstated interest in the project failing. Should you succeed against the odds, you are likely to win few friends and convert few waverers.

Convince the partnership before addressing the outside world.

Suppliers who understand lawyers

If you consider how hard it can be for the outside world to understand the world of the law, and how hard it is for the lawyer to comprehend the world of marketing, then imagine the damage that can be caused by a lack of communication with suppliers. If you do not have an easy working relationship with your designer; if your printer reels off jargon to the partnership; if the stand designer treats the firm as if it were his smallest account; and if the advertising people want to spend £500 setting an advertisement into £600 of booked space – then you're in trouble.

Flexibility and time

Initiatives, if developed properly, need time in order to come to fruition. Martyn Gowar of Lawrence Graham believes that 'having been marketing partner here for three years, I am just beginning to win'. There are very few quick-grow promotional projects in a law firm.

Equally, partners and fee earners have to give time. This requires flexibility and commitment when planning and supporting promotional activities which have been evolved to meet marketing objectives.

A good budget

Most of the marketing budget falls into the fourth P – the subject of this book – promotion. But how big should that budget be? How can you set a figure, when you don't know what the business and marketing plans will suggest?

The brave firm waits for, and then costs, the recommended programmes. If the activity planned is necessary, the budget will be found. In many firms, such activity-driven budgeting is supplanted by the allocation of a figure plucked from the air.

Thus a good budget is one that allows the marketing plan to be carried through, from research to implementation to assessment. As a rule of thumb, this will entail allocating between 1 and 2% of turnover to promotional expenditure.

If marketing is viewed as an overhead, it is likely that promotional initiatives will be dismissed on the grounds of expense. It is the marketing-oriented firm which views promotional enterprise as a road to long-term benefits, which will invest bravely and imaginatively for a future pay-back.

Planning

This is one of the most important words in the marketing lexicon. Without planning, huge wastage can, and does, occur. Kim Tasso, who wrote prolifically on marketing techniques when Director of Marketing at Nabarro Nathanson, bemoaned the professions' lack of campaign planning and strategic thinking. This ranged across the means and the end – from ignorance of flow charts to confusion over objectives.

Obviously, planning starts with the Plans – business and marketing. These need to be succinct, practical documents of perhaps half a dozen pages. Too many marketing gurus write long, complicated, clever documents, which bamboozle and fail to come to clear, simple conclusions.

Planning should permeate every stage from strategic thinking to promotional enactment. At Ince & Co, Georgina Schneeman has transformed major clients into a series of 18 month plans. In each case, a single partner has responsibility for carrying out planned activities over this period. Schedules, charts and checklists then police programmes of planned activity.

Only this level of forward thinking will enable the firm to control client contact on the promotional side. Activities will be generated to meet needs. The prevalent alternative is the evolution of activities, followed by the desperate attempt to fit clients to that activity.

Staff resources

Both of those quoted above feel that more could be made of existing staffing within law firms. Kim Tasso wants to see legal secretaries, many of whom are highly qualified, used more imaginatively, while Georgina Schneeman is concerned at the inability of some partners to delegate. In his tour of firms, while researching this book, the author saw too many underused fee earners, bored secretaries and sleepy trainee solicitors to disagree.

It is not necessary to empire-build in a law firm. The marketing department (or PR office, or promotion service, or marketing communications section) can function fairly happily with perhaps four full time staff in a large firm, three in a medium sized firm, and one or two in a small firm. However, more important than weight of numbers is availability of short-term support in the event of a) a large project and b) a crisis.

Campaigns

If initiatives are undertaken in isolation, the potential gain is minimised. It is far better to target a sector, then to plan and undertake a series of promotional activities in order to achieve the goal of winning client business in that sector.

Mutual understanding

Allusions have already been made to the cultural differences between the marketing professional and the lawyer. In addition to overcoming these differences, it is vital that the role of each in the marketing process be understood.

ASSESSING & ENACTING PROMOTIONAL IDEAS

Fig 7

THE IDEA

	THE PARTNER	THE CLIENT	THE MARKETEER	THE BUDGET	THE STRATEGY
FEASIBILITY	IS THERE A PARTNER TO ACT AS CHAMPION?	IS THIS OF INTEREST & POTENTIAL BENEFIT TO CLIENTS?	ARE PROMOTIONAL RESOURCES AVAILABLE?	IS THERE A BUDGET?	DOES THIS IDEA FIT THE BUSINESS & MARKETING STRATEGY?
PLANNING	MAKES DECISIONS ATTENDS MEETINGS DELEGATES/FINDS HELP	INITIATION OF CLIENT RESEARCH AS REQUIRED	DRAWS UP TIMETABLE PREPARES ACTIVITIES SETS OBJECTIVES	SET ACCURATE COSTS	CAN THE IDEA BE EXTENDED OR FURTHER DEVELOPED?
ENACTION	ALLOCATES TIME REMAINS AVAILABLE AUTHORISES ACTIVITIES INFORMS & INVOLVES PARTNERS	GAUGE INTEREST AND ENTHUSIASM	CONDUCTS PROGRAMME INFORMS & INVOLVES PARTNERSHIP	MONITOR SPEND INCURRED	CHECK ACTIVITIES CONTINUE TO CONFORM TO STRATEGY
ASSESSMENT	REPORTS TO PARTNERS	RESEARCH CLIENT IMPACT	CHECKS IF RESULTS MET OBJECTIVES	VALUE FOR MONEY?	HAVE STRATEGIC AIMS BEEN MET OR FURTHERED?

In the case of promotional activity, as in all aspects of marketing, the marketeer is there to help, not to take on tasks in isolation. Unless this is accepted, progress and success are likely to prove elusive. The partner or fee earner is the product, the service, the core of what is being offered to clients. Unless integrally involved, the firm's offer will appear insubstantial or hollow.

Matthew Fuller, marketing manager at Wilde Sapte, explains this by stating that 'the marketer can only advise and help to create the right environment for the business — it is up to the lawyer to go out ... and satisfy the client'. He sees part of the marketing professional's role as being an information exchange, knowing what is happening throughout a firm and disseminating that knowledge. Georgina Schneeman encapsulates the position as 'counsellor and facilitator'.

This is not to say that all those who fall within the scope of the 'marketeer' title have no practical function. On the contrary, as this book seeks to show, they run the promotional mechanism. However, they can only do so effectively when working alongside a sleeves-rolled up lawyer.

As David Mosey, a partner of Trowers & Hamlins observes, 'there is something quite touching in the naivety with which apparently hard bitten lawyers have handed over problems to PR and marketing consultants, expecting them to provide unilateral, fairytale solutions'.

It is of course equally important, that the marketing employee or consultant understands how lawyers work, think and wish to use marketing. Only through an awareness of what has gone wrong in the past can progress be made in the future. Part of what went wrong was mutual misunderstanding. Thus those involved in promoting law firms would do well to clearly communicate their intentions and the *modus operandi* of a marketeer within the firm.

The right stuff

There are few tougher areas of marketing communications than the legal market. A group of lawyers represents one of the most conservative, intelligent and demanding audiences anyone could wish to persuading. Being relatively new to the disciplines of marketing, they are not only likely to need convincing, but also constant reassuring, coercing and directing. That demands a certain type of professional. Without natural authority, expertise, self belief and presentation skills, patience, humour and (this is an honest book) low cunning, few ideas will get off the ground.

A client perspective

Fortunately, the once bewildering imprecation to 'look from the client's point of view' appears to have been largely accepted within law firms. However, it has yet to achieve wholesale translation in marketing and promotional terms.

As long ago as 1984, Wally Olins wrote in Marketing Legal Services that 'nobody will ... understand what (solicitors) do if they use obfuscating and imprecise language such as this'. He was referring to a list of services offered by solicitors. This ran, in part: Agricultural property; Employment; European Human Rights; Copyright – and so forth.

Much has changed in a decade, but one will still find such lists. Frankly, a lack of space often makes such terseness unavoidable. However, Olins' point was presumably that lawyers believed – if they ever thought about it at all – that everyone would understand what was meant by such shorthand.

The overriding impression is that it is up to the client to ask, not for the lawyer to explain. The mystique is carefully guarded, at the expense of clarity and helpful detail.

This is but a small and imprecise example. There are many more, but it is unfair to dwell on the negative. The ground is shifting rapidly. It is encouraging that more and more lawyers are moving to a client-centred approach, and thus providing true service.

A client-centred approach affects all aspects of the firm's business, not just the promotional side of marketing. Meetings are configured and run to provide what the client wants; correspondence considers what the client needs to understand, not merely what the lawyer wants to report. Client orientation is an easy shift to administer, but requires an enormous initial leap of imagination and commitment.

Knowledge of clients and contacts

What is the end purpose of marketing and promotional effort? Obviously, to win more business. So who are the targets? Clients and client referrers.

To be honest, the promotional role does not necessitate vast knowledge of the client profile. That is a core marketing task. However, since promotional activity will be used to reach the target audience (a jargon phrase which is readily deciphered), it is helpful to understand the scope of a firm's useful contacts (as shown in Fig 1 on p 3).

Running in-house promotional services

The following are of debatable (though the author believes significant) importance in establishing the ground for effective promotional work within a firm of solicitors:

- Keep everyone involved in promotional work in the same open plan office. It is important that individuals pick up information by osmosis. Do not relegate assistants or secretaries to a separate room.
- Put a single partner (or marketing director) in charge of day to day decision making, relating to marketing, promotional and PR matters. Hold bi-weekly or monthly meetings with a steering committee. These meetings should be held to keep the partnership informed, to receive guidance and feedback.
- Make sure that the promotional service is provided by more doers than thinkers. Most successful promotional activity requires substantial administrative support.
- Invest in the right technological tools: there is no point employing a senior marketing professional or an expensive consultant if you are going to land him or her with a database that does not work, a printer that can't produce long mail merges, inadequate facilities or software for newsletter production, or equipment on which to produce visual aids (slides, overhead projection acetates, etc).
- Ensure that the promotional professional meets and speaks to all partners and fee earners regularly. Create a speaker slot at the annual conference; set up regular fee earner lunches where marketing and public relations can be explained and differentiated and where individuals can be told how they can contribute on the firm's behalf.
- Employ only people who are prepared to follow a day spent carry ing boxes around an exhibition with a day stuffing envelopes. Much of the day to day work is boring. Potential prima donnas should be avoided at all costs.

2 Corporate identity

Those who claim not to have a corporate identity are merely acknowledging that they have no control over how they portray themselves to the outside world.

According to Neil Morgan of the Cardiff Business School, 'corporate or firm image is the perception of the reality of the firm held in the minds of its clients, competitors, potential marketplace and other relevant "publics".'

Put more succinctly, it is the perceived personality or performance of an organisation.

It could also be argued – it should be argued – that the partners and staff of the firm have a right to be included as a relevant 'public', whose perception of the firm's personality forms a constituent part of the identity. This is always provided that these views are not mistakenly considered to reflect the true personality of the firm.

That personality is comprised of several elements.

To the client a firm's identity comprises of perceived service quality, price, value and so forth. Additionally, impressions are gained from the people within an organisation, which is judged by the individual personalities (and appearance) of its personnel.

Then there is the architecture, colour, decor and style of the offices, and the fixtures and furnishings. Design consultant Wally Olins has described legal offices as 'for the most part, unfriendly, intimidating, alienating, strange and remote from everyday life'. One may not altogether agree with Mr Olins, but it would be foolish not to find out if his views were shared. If this is a prevalent view, a corporate identity programme provides the perfect opportunity to rectify the situation.

Finally, all publicity and promotional activities, stationery, IT-generated forms and professional documentation are elements of the corporate identity.

The sum total of all the subjects discussed in this book make an important contribution to a firm's corporate identity. A brochure, proposal document or even advertisement may have to represent the firm, perhaps helping to sway appointment decisions.

Why bother?

No one would pretend that seeing three different but linked manifestations of an organisation would unilaterally lead to business wins. However, it would be a brave battler against the tide who felt it made no difference whether promotional tools looked consistent or not. As Neil Morgan goes on to say, 'a well conceived and successfully implemented corporate identity programme can increase the likelihood of potential clients gaining and retaining name awareness ... being asked to take part in a beauty parade, make a presentation or give a proposal'.

The importance of a homogenous and appropriate identity is tied directly to the importance an organisation places in itself as a single entity. If the culture states that the firm is simply a loose pooling of entrepreneurs, the need for a strong central identity diminishes.

However, even such an organisation would lay claim to certain features – quality of service perhaps – held in common by all of its practitioners. It would expect the outside world to form a favourable view of the organisation as well as its constituent parts. It would hope that a stamp of approval against one person would serve to endorse another.

Therefore a coherent identity matters to such an entity barristers chambers, for example. If a set of chambers is actively trying to appear united, the need for communicating common values can hardly be overstressed.

Hence the need for attention being paid to shaping and controlling a corporate identity. Too often, this is seen as something that will take care of itself. Control takes time, attention and the occasional temper tantrum. Lawrence Graham's Martyn Gowar confesses to 'becoming extremely angry' whenever stipulations are side-stepped.

The alternatives

A brochure may be produced by one office, elements of which are integrated into an exhibition stand. A partner asks to have her business cards customised. Another wants the logo made bigger on a publication promoting his specialisation. 'I want to get rid of that horrible motif as well. I can't stand it.' So it goes.

The upshot is a welter of unrelated imagery, different typefaces and apparently unconnected visual material. The onlooker seeing two items of promotional material together will not be able to relate the two as from the same firm. Worse, the message may be one of confusion. An organisation which cannot communicate its identity does not inspire confidence in its overall management.

This focuses on the negative. Just as its absence reflects badly, the use of a properly controlled corporate identity lends positive attributes to a firm. It speaks of professionalism. It looks planned. It implies consistent quality across a breadth of service – implying range rather than limitation.

And it makes life easier! No more disputes about how something should look. The establishment of an identity leads to agreed ways of doing things. As Lynn Hill of Taylor Joynson Garrett found, 'where once we saw endless struggling over colours and identity, now there is no question as to which is the correct approach'.

Uniformity or total change

Establishing corporate identity may be about creating uniformity, or it may entail more substantial change. The argument for the latter is more difficult to win, particularly if the substance of that argument derives from within the organisation. Change can only be justified if it leads to a visual identity better reflecting to attributes wanted by clients. For example, simply bringing the form into the 1990s is no use at all. unless greater modernity is known to be required by clients and the existing identity is known to look old-fashioned. This research is usually a prerequisite when a wholesale change in corporate identity is envisaged. It provides the only valid argument to overcome innate conservatism and justify the cost of the exercise.

Finding your consultant

So, having decided you want to embark on this road to consistency, how do you find someone to help?

Because the cultural divide between supplier and lawyer can be enormous, it is wise to find a design consultant who has worked with a law firm in the past. Asking opposite numbers in friendly firms, or your marketing manager, is the best way to find the right people for the job.

It isn't necessarily the best option to go to the corporate identity specialists, unless you want the exercise gilded and built to Rolls Royce specifications. You'll get experience and perhaps a tip top job, but you'll pay through the nose and probably spend as much on the manual (beautifully produced in doe-skin) which stipulates rules on the identity as you'd budgeted for the entire job. Jennie Gubbins of Trowers & Hamlins offer the following advice 'never accept anything that fails to meet your requirements exactly. Find a designer who can tailor creativity to your stated objectives rather than his or her preconceived ideas.

Any designer has the skills necessary to produce an identity. The right one is the one who best responds to the detailed brief you produce.

The best course of initial action is to produce a highly detailed brief. Time devoted to this is time well spent. An hour dedicated to getting this right can save hundreds of wasted hours and thousands of pounds. Because you will not have done this before, because the designer won't know your firm, and because a corporate identity exercise can be as extensive or restricted as you like, a clear brief may be the best form of control you can have. (See the end of this chapter for guidance on what might fall within the brief).

Select no more than four or five designers to pitch for the identity review. Telephone them first, to ensure that they are willing to be considered and to produce work for a pitch on a speculative basis.

Send each a copy of the brief, along with copies of all existing material which will be subject to review. Invite each designer in to meet you and discuss the brief in more detail.

Set and circulate a timetable, so that all parties (partners and designers) are aware of what is required, and by when.

Although every partner and member of the firm will have an interest in (and decided views on) any changes being proposed, it is essential that a small group of senior people steer through the review. This sub-committee should number no more than four people. Many more and the initiative will sink amidst cross-firing cannons.

Timetable and costings

Once each designer has pitched against the brief to the firm, it should be possible to set your priorities on terms of implementing the new identity. This may be dictated by immediate needs, natural opportunities to replace old stocks, politics, or simply your budget.

Once a timetable is in place, and before any great expense is incurred, the designer should provide rough guidelines on costs incurred in fulfilling the timetable obligations (unless a full budget has already been agreed).

Because the goalposts will inevitably shift, and because elements of the identity will still need to be agreed or refined, these costings should not be seen by either party as final. However, it should be made clear that it is up to the designer to apprise the firm of costs incurred, additional expenditure necessitated, and changes to the originally anticipated budget.

If at any time you find yourself uncertain as to what costs are being incurred, have been incurred, or can be anticipated, stop the process until your mind has been set at rest. There is no rush. Far better to let the timetable slip than to lose faith in the process because you and your designer are talking at cross-purposes (inevitably to your financial disadvantage).

Certainty of purpose: the essential ingredient

Corporate identity changes are painful at the best of times. Unless the process is set up to be transparent, and unless all expenditure shocks are averted, insuperable problems can develop.

One other caveat: a corporate identity exercise is not primarily a creative process. Creativity must be subordinated to the need to convey appropriate messages to the outside world. Unless these attributes appeal to actual and potential clients, and reflect the way the firm really is (rather than wants to be), 'creative' may come to mean 'cosmetic'.

The goal

At the end of every exercise, however extensive or restricted, you will be looking for a greater degree of uniformity in the way the firm is presented. Crucial is a viable, simple means of perpetuating changes made. You will need clearly comprehensible documentation, which shows exactly how formats should be used, layouts established, typefaces varied, headlines and copy spaced and colours and materials specified.

The corporate identity manual

Corporate identity manuals have been known to fall into disuse, and even disrepute. The reason, as is so often the case in marketing and promotional initiatives, often lies in overegging the pudding. Vast tomes have been produced by designers who'd mastered the art of establishing identities, but who have no idea of how a professional firm operates – or how a layman reads.

A corporate identity manual needs to be simple and consistent. If necessary, it should be produced in two forms: the version for the law firm to read and refer to, and the technical specifications for use by designers, printers and the like.

The manual should be used by anyone who produces visual material on the firm's behalf, and for those who police the identity. Consideration should be given to whether the manual should be loose leaf and copyable, or produced in several master versions.

The manual should lay down stipulations to cover specific items, while providing guidance in more general areas. To take a specific and common example, the manual would address the following areas in a corporate brochure:

- Dimensions of the publication.
- Typesizes and typefaces to be used.
- Print materials and any special treatment (marbling, embossing, laminating etc).
- Colour references (known as 'pantones') to specify corporate and other colours used.
- Layout of pages, specifying such matters as the balance between text and illustrations, size of margins, location of page numbers and headings.
- Use of the firm's name/logo.
- Use of any additional brochure attributes (eg photography reproduction or any special print processes).

The successful manual determines certain things but leaves some aspects to creative interpretation. A straitjacket will always be fought against. If the precise location of an image on the page is set in stone, for example, the nature of that image should still be open to minor variation.

If correctly established and applied, a corporate identity manual will lead to a balanced consistency in the firm's visual identity. Merely sending a copy to an office overseas, a stand designer or even an interior decorator should achieve this goal.

Thus when the firm's umbrella, brochures, pencils, notepaper, letterhead, business card – indeed any publication or production – appear together in an office or on a display, their common 'look' signifies disciplined production and a professional approach.

Economies of scale

A consistent corporate identity also allows economies of scale in production. Any form of rationalisation has management implications in terms of cost savings. While long term economies of scale should not be anticipated as a justification for short term spending on a corporate identity review, they may help sell the concept to the doubters.

Law firms have distinctive but nebulous personalities. As entities, some are still pulling together, having spent centuries as the sum of distinct parts. The idea of departments and cross-selling is still (relatively) new. As such, a corporate identity exercise help to shape, rather than simply reflect, the way the firm imagines the outside world sees it – and how it sees itself.

In writing about corporate identity for architects, Lynne Choona Ryness observes that a new corporate identity 'often provides a stimulus for a practice to consider what it wants, where it is going and how it wishes to be perceived'.

The IT aspect

A full scale corporate identity exercise should always include information technology. If it does not, the only valid reason is a lack of appropriate technology, a limited budget or a differed application.

The firm's logo can be scanned into computer software, so that all internally produced documentation (proposals, fax headers etc) not only reflects the common identity, but does so consistently. If you are producing a new, consistent letterhead, it seems a waste to have the layout subject to the different interpretation of each secretary. Grids can be programmed into the IT systems, so that each letter can only be configured to the house style.

A final justification

Jeremiahs will still wonder why anyone should bother. Clients, who receive communications from more than one member of a firm, will usually provide the answer. If anyone thinks to ask them.

The corporate identity brief

The brief should include a description of the firm's clients together with an injunction that the firm's identity must attract and appeal to these clients. In addition, the brief should dictate exactly what you do and do not want done.

In addition, before talking to designers, you should agree and then list what elements need to be addressed by the corporate identity review.

General

- The firm's name (typeface, typestyle, typesize).
- Any additional visual identifier (the logo).
- Corporate colour(s).
- Acceptable typefaces and typestyles for text.
- Layout stipulations common to all manifestations of the identity.
- Print materials.

Stationery

- Letterhead.
- Continuation sheets.
- Compliment slips.
- Business cards.
- Envelopes.
- Mailing labels.
- Prepaid envelopes.
- Franking.
- Memorandum sheets (if preprinted).
- Invoices.
- Press release paper.
- Fax header sheets (if preprinted).
- All pro formas.
- Meeting room pads.
- Document covers.

Promotional materials

- Firm's brochure.
- Brochures promoting specific services or markets.
- Graduate recruitment brochure.
- Vacation work literature.
- Newletters.
- Bulletins/Information publications.
- Any other publications.
- Proposal documents.
- Proposal wallets.
- Presentation folders.
- Advertisements (corporate, specialist and recruitment).
- Exhibition stands.
- Christmas cards.

- Map cards.
- Invitation cards.
- Posters.
- Video or TV images.
- Slides or overhead projector images.
- 'Merchandise' (pencils, pens, umbrellas, t-shirts, other give-aways).

Information technology

- Incorporation of corporate identity layout and formats in all documents produced.
- Templates for layout of all documents produced.

Office

- Colour schemes throughout building.
- Entrance and reception signage.
- Brochure display area.
- Meeting rooms (displays, colour of table baize, etc).
- Staff uniforms.

Summary

- Ensure that the proposed developments have the required support internally. This may necessitate patient lobbying or slow introduction of new elements. Whichever is the case, changes in a corporate identity can touch on delicate nerves. Make time to smooth feathers before they can get ruffled.
- Talk to marketeers from other law firms about their experiences, contacts and recommendations.
- Determine your objective: is it evolution or revolution?
- Consider what you hope to include in a review. Decide whether you will be looking at items beyond stationery, publications and publicity materials. Examples might include design of the offices, or computing (creating software, scanning in logos, or gridding documents to achieve consistency with the identity).
- Liaise closely with all those who will be affected (such as those who look after IT software, or stationery).
- Establish specific requirements – is this just a question of designing parameters for future materials, or is immediate creation/print work needed?

CORPORATE IDENTITY

- Write a clear brief, stating your objectives. List the items referred to above, and list/describe any additional elements which may need to be created in the future. Send this brief to those invited to pitch.
- Compile a list of corporate identity consultants. Any designer will claim to be able to address the task. Ask colleagues in other firms for their advice. Use directories such as the Marketing Handbook. You will probably be spoilt for choice by the unprompted influx of promotional literature, offering appropriate services.
- Gather together examples of all items that need to be readdressed during the corporate identity review.
- Make time to meet those pitching, if they want to meet you (as they should) before drawing up proposals. Give them examples of the items collected together. Only by assessing what has gone before will they be in a position to recommend the next stage. It is highly unlikely that a complete change of direction will be taken in each element of the new identity; relics of the past will doubtless remain.
- Make sure all those asked to pitch receive the same information and are asked to present to the same level (ideas only/rough art-work/mocked up examples of materials).
- Arrange and hold presentations.
- Determine favoured choice against a checklist of requirements. Mark criteria out of 10. This will help resolve disputes over which supplier is favoured.
- Once an appointment has been made, establish a programme and timetable. Determine exactly what is and what is not covered in the review, how many copies of the manual you will be receiving, what is needed from you in the way of additional information, etc.
- Gauge likely costs and set budget limitations.
- Confirm timetable.
- Establish reporting system, whereby designer provides regular status updates (progress/costs).
- (Re-)cost the entire programme. Instruct the supplier that it is his or her responsibility to inform you of any increased costs arising during the programme, whether or not you initiate alterations or additions.
- Receive all elements of the firm's identity delineated in terms of layout, typeface, size, colour.
- Receive a manual, which sets and polices all stipulations regarding the corporate identity. Armed with the manual, you will be able to send copies along with a brief to a range of printers and designers when a job is imminent. Each will then be quoting against exactly

Fig 8

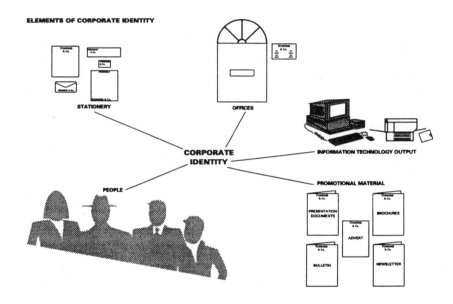

the same set specifications. There should be no room for misunder-standings, or for quoting against different criteria. Therefore, the manual becomes more than just a stipulating tool; it allows you to control costs through tracking down good value service.
- Communicate progress within the firm, to ensure that no one produces material that conflicts with the common style.
- Remove all evidence of pre-review materials from the firm.

Hints and tips

- Go for something simple when agreeing a corporate colour. If you agree a bespoke colour, it will cause you agonies trying to apply it uniformly across different paper stocks.
- Eschew the more exotic paper stocks. Find stocks which are already in your corporate colour(s), or a surface onto which your printer is confident of overprinting your colours accurately. Marbled or absorbent covers, for example, may lead to variation in production colour.
- Keep everything as simple as possible.

3 Advertising

Lawyers' advertising to date

Most advertising has taken one of five courses.

- Investment in large, corporate advertisements, then a sudden cutback when work has not arisen.
- A series of irregular small black and white advertisements, hidden apologetically in trade publications.
- 'Tombstone' advertising (small announcements, usually clustered together on the page), trumpeting the elevation of fee earners to the partnership, the opening of new offices, or involvement in major deals.
- Very little activity.
- Planned campaigns, where a consistent message appears consistently in various media, reflecting the same message being conveyed through other promotional activities.

It does not take a Saatchi to work out which of the above has most to recommend it, as a general approach to advertising.

Why should you advertise?

Why indeed? It is expensive and confusing. Why not avoid it altogether?

Lynn Hill of Taylor Joynson Garrett considers all advertising to be 'a colossal waste of money particularly when budgets are limited'. Grudgingly, she will admit to doing a little charity advertising, and spending money on supporting other initiatives, such as opening a new office. She may also be swayed by something obviously well targeted – a flier in Lloyds List to promote a shipping seminar, for example – but not by a full page corporate advertisement.

Sarah Dean, until recently Marketing Manager at Ashurst Morris Crisp, reckons to turn down 90% of advertising opportunities and only to consider advertising if there is an event that needs a publicity boost.

A page in the Financial Times might cost £25,000 before production costs. Why throw such a lot of money around, when it could be better spent elsewhere?

Such suspicion is probably healthy, provided that it does not develop into an irrational prejudice against all advertising. After all, you can place advertisements for hundreds rather than thousands of pounds. Even lawyers need to tell people what they are up to once in a while. As Edgar Howe stated, 'doing business without advertising is like winking at a girl in the dark: you know what you're doing, but nobody else does'.

Judiciously chosen, an advertising campaign can augment and publicise other marketing initiatives. After all, the medium works if it is used correctly. The key lies in making those judicious choices.

Basic guidelines

As with media relations (or for that matter, any form of promotions) so with advertising: there is no point taking space to say what you want to say, in a magazine where you want to be seen.

Start from the client's point of view.

Advertise something of interest to the epitome of the favoured client – and put the advertisement in something he or she reads.

What you want to say and what the client wants to hear should amount to the same thing. Often it does not. Many law firms waste money buying space in publications read by other lawyers, or in publications their clients don't read.

By all means advertise to other lawyers, but only if they are a deliberately chosen market – ie a potential source of new instructions.

Assuming you are aiming for the quality end of a market, it is preferable by far to pay twice as much to buy space in the sector-leading publication than to take advantage of the 20% discount in the also-ran.

Don't spread yourself across the entire range of sector publications. Focus on the most appropriate to your target clients.

But what do my clients read? Ask them. Simply by selecting a cross-section of amenable clients and asking them a few questions you could save yourself and the firm a lot of time, money and effort.

It is vital to set objectives. As Neil Morgan stresses, all the positives of an advertising campaign (awareness, image enhancement, confidence in service offerings, reaching a wide audience, differentiation, etc) only work 'if the campaign is properly planned, targeted, designed and executed, with a sufficient budget and over an appropriate length of time'.

Part of the problem facing those deciding where to advertise is the plethora of options. In even the most esoteric field, you may find specialist periodicals, academic journals, lightweight magazines and general publications with sections devoted to the field. It is tempting to throw your hand in with the name you know or the biggest in the sector – or even to favour a particular advertising representative, who scores points by calling you a firm and not a company.

For a professional firm, size is not everything. If you are a construction lawyer, you may discover that 33,000 people receive *Chartered Builder* 10 times a year, while 37,000 get *Construction News* weekly. Ten issues of *Professional Builder* are received by 121,000 people each year, while *Construction Law*'s six issues reach perhaps between 1-2,000. There are maybe a dozen other interesting-looking publications in the sector. Which is the right publication for you?

Ignore the quantity and focus on quality. Since you are trying to reach decision makers, in advertising you do not need to broadcast – merely to target.

Therefore, ring the advertising department of each publication and ask for a media pack. This will include a recent copy of the magazine, details of circulation and recipient profile. Check if the publication is free or requested by subscription. A free publication sent to a heavyweight audience may not be read. A handful of subscribers is worth a bushel of people who bin their issue on arrival.

Look at the quality of editorial – and the quality of advertiser. If two or three competitors are already there, they are unlikely to have chosen blind.

Ring colleagues, in your firm and in others. Find the consensus view. It is rare that this will be universal, but it should become clearer. Every publication can offer a good reason to advertise; if this were not so, it would have gone to the wall. Therefore, since it is always easy to justify a decision to advertise in a particular publication, it is lazy not to present corroborating evidence that it is indeed the right place.

Should you advertise against a special feature, or in isolation?

The most effective advertising is usually repetitive. A campaign running in several publications over several months is likely to be noticed. A one off may sink without trace.

A logical time to advertise on a one off basis is the special feature, run by a publication as a focus on a specific industry, product or service. The advantage is that there is a good chance the people in that field will read the feature. Often, publications arrange special mailings to organisations working in the area covered by the feature.

The rationale for these special features is to sell advertising. Your competitors will all be contacted. The result will be a plethora of advertising alongside a range of articles. Your small black and white advertisement will disappear.

It is probably only beneficial to take advertising alongside such a feature if either you cannot afford not to be there, or if you spend enough money to appear prominently (full colour and/or full page). A small advertisement may make you look like a small player. Alternatively, consider whether there are any other ways of standing out. Discuss adding a bound-in or loose insert to the publication. These can be highly effective within special reports and features.

If your budget is very limited, it may be better to avoid the crowded special feature and aim for a position in a different issue of the publication. Talk to the advertising department and find out what editorial is planned next time around. You may have to pay a premium to book a specific location, but this presents an opportunity for imaginative buying – and cost-effective advertising.

What to say

The style of recent legal advertising has created a gulf between the sophisticated and the mundane. That does not mean to say that sophisticated is necessarily best.

Copywriting is a specialist art. It is not an easy life. As Aldous Huxley once said, 'it is far easier to write ten passably effective sonnets than one effective advertisement'.

If you expect to invest heavily in advertising, hire a copywriter. If you do not, there is one vital rule to follow:

Get rid of all those words.

The temptation is to bombard limited space with text. You will have a pleasant, warm feeling when you have shoehorned every pertinent phrase and bullet point into the advertisement. No one will read it, because it is impenetrable, but at least you've satisfied every partner that their specialisation is covered.

This is where anyone with knowledge about advertising earns their corn. Massaging egos while persuading fluently, he recommends an alternative approach. He treads the fine line between humour and crassness, the eye-catching and the irrelevant, in seeking a headline and copy which will captivate the reader in the millisecond before the page is turned.

Let us start with the headline. Its purpose is to catch the eye. If it merely refers to the firm's name, or bland subject matter, it is a dead line. If it alludes to something likely to be of interest to the reader, it has some merit. However, in order to function as it is intended, it needs to have something extra. That element can rarely be specified. What should be stipulated, however, is that it should be written with the reader's point of view in mind.

This simple point would, if generally adopted, change the face of professional practice advertising. Look through any selection of copy and vast quantities are drafted with headlines that are the advertising equivalent of the most boring person you could meet at a party. See Figure 9 for a demonstration and Figure 10 as an alternative option.

Fig 9

TURGID

SEAL & WINSTON
—— SOLICITORS ——

LEGAL HELP WITH

RUNNING YOUR BUSINESS

SEAL & WINSTON HAS PROVIDED LEGAL ADVICE TO BUSINESSES IN THE WEST MIDLANDS FOR TWENTY YEARS. WE COVER A FULL RANGE OF SERVICES, FROM SETTING UP A COMPANY TO FUNDING AND FROM DIRECTORS' DUTIES TO EMPLOYEES' CONTRACTS.

WE CAN ADVISE ON CONTRACTUAL MATTERS, DEBT RECOVERY, GENERAL LITIGATION AND ALL PROPERTY ISSUES.

FOR A FREE INITIAL CONSULTATION, PLEASE CONTACT MIKE HENRY OR STELLA RUSH.

SEAL & WINSTON
1 PARK GARDENS
BIRMINGHAM BH2 1DR
Tel. 021 278 7171

Fig 10

MORE READABLE

SEAL & WINSTON
SOLICITORS

LEGAL ADVISORS TO WEST MIDLANDS BUSINESS

"MAY WE QUOTE YOU TOO?"

TO FIND OUT MORE ABOUT WHAT

WE CAN DO FOR YOUR BUSINESS

PLEASE CALL MIKE HENRY OR
STELLA RUSH
ON **021 278 7171**

"An all-round excellent service"
John James
Winston & Co.

"Legal advice of the highest calibre"
Mary Smale
Smale's Industries

"Your firm sets and achieves the highest standards"
Laurie Rylands
LMR Ltd.

"Thank you for your courteous service"
Frank Adams
Metroways plc

Think client

Advertising approaches will vary, depending on the firm, the publication and its readership. Permeating all decisions should be an awareness of the client's interest rather than what the firm wants to say. In the main part of the text (the body copy), one or two points will be made succinctly, maybe abstractly, possibly gnomically.

A cartoon, line drawing or even full colour illustration or photograph may provide the optical attraction, balanced by the text. If not, the text will be laid out professionally, to stand out from the cobbled together advertisements destined to jostle for attention on the page.

And - it bears repetition - it will only stand out if it has lost its burden of words.

Will it be read? Possibly. Will it be noticed? Maybe. Will any impact result in the reader's mind?

You read magazines and newspapers. With the exception of the largest, most frequently seen print advertisements, most of us would be hard pressed to recall any messages we have seen recently. Yet, fight the thought though we may, the message gets through to us, subliminally or otherwise.

Response mechanism

Interestingly, research shows that recall among readers rises if a response mechanism is built into an advertisement, and if a cost/fee is quoted. Certainly, the former option is recommended.

A coupon provides feedback to show whether what is offered is wanted by the readers of the publication. It functions only when a product or service is on offer, so militates against pure hype in an advertisement. It also provides solid information, showing which respondents are interested in which services the firm can provide.

However, even if coupons can provide a measurable response, it is wise not to expect too much from your advertising. As the industry itself acknowledges, the message is largely insidious. Most advertising is not noticed consciously.

Reinforcement

Often, the only chance this shadowy recollection has of rooting into the subconscious lies in reinforcement. If enough similar messages are received, an impression is formed in the memory. Thus, advertising usually only works by repetition (ie a campaign) or in tandem with other forms of promotion.

Factual or creative? Regular or occasional?

As has been noted, some firms run campaigns (see Figure 11), while others look for the occasional opportunity to run alongside pertinent editorial coverage, which acts to reinforce (and lend authority to) the advertising. Some produce four-colour full page copywritten advertisements, while others ask the publication to typeset their one colour text within quarter-page confines. Some provide screeds of facts, while others convey their message through abstractions. One firm may have an advertising budget while another may allocate money on a case by case basis.

One might have strong views, but it is impossible to state definitively which is the right course. The amateurs are bemused and the professionals divided. Everyone has a view on advertising, and those clients who swear by high impact, creative and targeted advertisements are balanced by those who think such activities inappropriate for their lawyers. Doubtless, the pretentious and the inept are unacceptable, but there is a wealth of room in between.

However, the points stressed at the end of this chapter are generally accepted, and should be adopted automatically, unless there is a substantial and specific contrary argument.

General guidelines

When considering advertising, some rather obvious points need to be made.

When you buy space, that is all you buy. You still need to generate copy, visuals if appropriate, a design, typesetting and artwork. At least, someone does.

The simplest advertisement is one colour (almost invariably black) text. If the publication is prepared to set the copy all you need do is supply it and specify any layout stipulations. A sketch or an example of a previous advertisement should suffice to set matters in train.

But what about typeface and typesize?

How will the publication reproduce your logo?

THE ROLE OF ADVERTISING IN A TYPICAL CAMPAIGN

Fig 11

	JAN	FEB	MAR	APR	MAY	JUNE	JULY	AUG	SEPT	OCT	NOV	DEC
ADVERTISING	●		●		●	●		●		●		●
NEWSLETTER CIRCULATED			●			●			●			●
PROMOTIONAL PUBLICATIONS PRINTED		●					●					
DIRECT MAILING			●					●				
SEMINAR HELD				●					●			
CONFERENCE & EXHIBITION ATTENDED											●	
ARTICLE IN PRESS				●				●				●

Advertising annotations:
- JAN — WITH RESPONSE MECHANISM TO GAUGE INTEREST
- MAR — TO PROMOTE SEMINAR
- MAY — TO MAINTAIN MOMENTUM
- JUNE — TO MAINTAIN MOMENTUM
- AUG — TO SUPPORT ARTICLE IN PRESS AND TO PROMOTE SEMINAR
- OCT — TO PUBLICISE EXHIBITION ATTENDANCE
- DEC — WITH RESPONSE MECHANISM TO GAUGE INTEREST

How can you check that mistakes are not made during the typesetting?

Many organisations have strict guidelines on the layout of advertisements, down to the positioning of the logo, the relative scale of the typography, and the fonts to be used. If you ask the publication in which your advertisement is to appear to create your layout, you may be able to suggest, but you won't be able to control.

Sending a bromide (artwork) of your logo is not the same as sending camera ready artwork of the entire advertisement, set to the dimensions of the space booked.

Although you will be entitled to check and amend proofs, you will lose quality control and have less leverage in putting wrongs right.

Professional help

Thus, for anything but the simplest advertisements, it is preferable to use a designer and/or typesetter to retain creative control. For cheap, straightforward advertisements, however, their share of the cost would be out of proportion to the expenditure entailed. For a more complex or large-scale creation, they represent money well spent.

Traditional wisdom has it that production costs amount to approximately 10% of space booking costs. This is the sort of figure which seriously misleads most advertisers. Production is mostly a one-off cost, while space booked may encompass many publications. Thus a £50,000 advertising campaign might justify £5,000 of location photography, copywriting, typesetting, production of artwork and assorted models' time, but a lesser campaign could hardly bear or justify such costs.

The simple fact is that there is no rule of thumb. Space costs can be found easily in a directory such as BRAD, but production costs will depend entirely on the sophistication of the effect you want to achieve and how much quality control you require.

Start with a designer

A good, creative designer will be happy to take responsibility for the concept of an advertisement or campaign, as well as doing typesetting and layout work. You or a copywriter will need to provide the text and contribute to the conceptual thinking. The designer also produces finished artwork, incorporating images and typeset text, to be forwarded to the publication.

If you employ an advertising or PR agency, they will either have design, setting, copywriting and media buying resources in-house, or will be able to put together and manage the entire package. They are likely to mark up costs passed on to clients by around 17.5%. Agencies should be entitled to discounts on space booked (usually 10%). If you employ the agency, make sure that this discount is passed to you ie that you are not charged the published price for space.

However, agency involvement, intended to save you time and add creativity, may do nothing of the sort. Meetings, contrary intentions and misunderstandings often make it easier to generate and place occasional advertising yourself, unless you are looking at a lot of complex and specialised work. Figure 12 outlines the quality, cost and difficulty implications of your final choice.

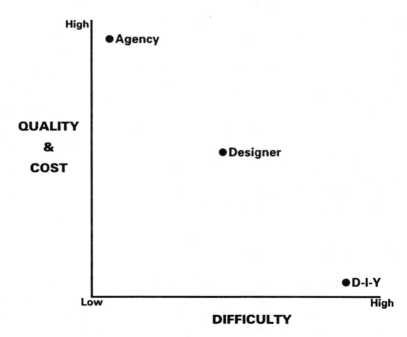

Fig 12

What to look for

Consider using a small design company, or a freelance. Don't employ specialist typesetters to do your design and layout work, unless they have a specialist design arm.

Look for a designer who has typesetting facilities which can handle your corporate typeface, and who doesn't charge for his or her own errors in setting copy. Provide copy and a hypothetical brief for contenders to quote against. Ask for a written indication of how you will be charged (against a clock, by word count, by job definition?). Charging for creative work is notoriously difficult, but so is paying for inflated self-worth: find out how such creativity is measured and billed.

More important than cost is quality. Every designer has a portfolio. Ask to see examples of previous work. You don't need a carbon copy of what you hope to achieve – merely an indication that the standard is high, the presentation professional, the work cost-effective, and that the individual is someone with whom you can do business.

Steps along the way

You might become involved in an advertising transaction in any number of ways. However, a hypothetical but typical advertising transaction might entail the following:

- Receive notification from a publication's advertising department of an editorial feature covering an area in which you specialise.
- Notify whoever looks after media relations, to investigate opportunities to write for the feature.
- You (gain authority to) book space. You determine the dimensions and mechanical details of space taken/publication. Establish copy date.
- Commission/write and agree copy, to conform to layout, wording and 'house-style' dictates.
- Instruct designer/typesetter to set copy to specified style and space dictates. Give artificially early deadline, to allow for delays.
- Check and agree/amend setting. Authorise finished artwork once setting is correct.
- Deliver camera ready artwork to the publication prior to copy deadline.

Selectivity

Advertising can be expensive. A page in a low circulation and low-profile magazine might cost £500: in a national broadsheet it could be 20 or even 50 times that. On top are the production costs. It is important, therefore, to advertise selectively.

Support areas of your firm's business that are growing, show long term potential, where you expect to recruit, and where partners are keen to market expertise. In other words, don't advertise in isolation; use such promotion to supplement other marketing activities.

It is worth stressing the point that a one-off advertisement may have impact, but several advertisements in consecutive issues of a publication are more likely to fix themselves in the mind of the reader. This is a case where the whole is often worth more than the sum of its constituent parts.

TV, radio, video, posters

Advertising on television and radio will only appeal to firms with a strong regional or local presence. Being expensive, both need to justify their cost through effectively targeting the audience sought by the firm. National television and radio cannot achieve such targeting.

However, some firms have experimented with regional television and local radio, often bought at off-peak rates to reach specific markets. Promoting local conveyancing, personal injury or industrial illness services for example, has successfully converted new clients. Whether or not it has proved cost-effective remains the secret of the few who have tested the water.

In 1990, for example, Philip Hamer & Co became one of the first firms to try television advertising. They claimed more than 100 respondents generated by £15,000 of off-peak, discounted Yorkshire TV advertising. Recent TV advertising, according to Philip Hamer, has proved cheaper in terms of cost for response than print advertising.

The *Law Society Gazette* of 22 June 1994 reported that one regional television station, keen to attract solicitor's advertising, was offering to make a 30 second advertisement and provide sufficient air time to reach half of the local audience for a package price of £20,000.

Some professional firms have used electronic services such as Prestel, Oracle or Ceefax to promote themselves. This is imaginative but as yet there is no evidence to demonstrate the efficiency of such a vehicle.

Outside the legal fraternity, a favourite publicity tool used by businesses who have major developments to announce is the video news release (VNR). This works in exactly the same way as a press release, by providing free footage for TV stations.

Some television companies and production companies will compile images of a firm, the cost of the exercise being defrayed by multiple use. Thus the stock footage might by used in a VNR, for viewing on an exhibition stand, on a loop in the firm's reception area, or as part of new business presentations.

For most firms, the high cost and uncertain benefits in terms of accurate client targeting mean that film and tape continue to represent a questionable return on investment.

Poster advertising is an unusual but interesting option, of relevance primarily to small firms with a limited geographical catchment area. Poster advertising has a good track record in promoting professional firms.

Directories

Taking a listing is seen by many as a form of advertising. Because such listings are often handled by different partners and support staff in a firm, it can be a hidden form.

Directory listings should be centralised and treated as part of the advertising budget. As with any other form of advertising, criteria should be set and adhered to, to ensure that every opportunity is not taken up. A listing may cost anything from £30 to several thousand. Unless control is established, anomalies will occur and money will be misspent.

Directories fall within three main sections: legal, market sector, and advertorial.

The first two provide straight listings (carrying varying degrees of information) and are split between those which deal with the legal market and those that offer firms opportunities to promote legal services in specific market sectors.

Legal directories

At present, the two most prominent paid for UK directories in the legal category are the Legal 500 (published by Legalease) and Chambers & Partners. In addition, there are opportunities to appear in compendia produced by Butterworths, Waterlows, The Lawyer's Diary, and a range of practice-specific publications. International firms will be tempted by Martindale Hubbell, the International Financial Law Review, Kimes, and a veritable welter of EC/Europe-specific, Continent or country-related and global publications.

Which ones should you be in? All those listed above have either been around long enough to have some value, or are suitably authoritative to require an entry, even if for negative reasons (I must be seen to be in). Yet each specialisation within each firm will be served, if that is the right word, by an equally dazzling array of 'opportunities'.

Choosing a non-legal directory

As always, it is a question of doing your research and ensuring that you are acting within the strategic boundaries set by your marketing plan. There is no point taking a directory entry as a token way of publicising a section of the firm. Promotional work is not supposed to be fairly spread throughout a firm. It must bunch up in key areas, so that it acquires a momentum that achieves more than the sum of its constituent parts. In other words, don't contemplate a directory entry in a market sector unless it is working in tandem with a concerted marketing effort in that area.

If your resources and budget are infinite, take every opportunity that comes your way. Then please offer me your job. In the real world, it is imperative to decide on a policy of what to accept and what to refuse, and on what grounds, as early as possible. Otherwise time will be wasted circulating information. No one will know on what grounds to select options, so arbitrary behaviour will become endemic.

Advertorial directories

Nowhere is this more important than in determining a response to the third wave of directories: the advertorial directory. These function by selling you the chance of writing editorial which is 'supported' by advertising. Don't be misled by the innocuous supporting role. In fact, it is the advertisement that drives the whole process in such publications. You will never be given the chance to write editorial without shelling out first.

There are a welter of guides, directories, manuals and assorted publications in this grouping. Each will purport to be the authority on their respective trade/market sectors. The sales call that comes in will run along these lines:

'Hello Mr/Ms (name). My name is xxxx and I am calling from (name of directory sponsor). I am sure you have heard of the (name of publication), which is sent to 30,000 of the leading decision makers in the (market sector).'

'We are offering only the most authoritative firms in this area the chance to write for the publication, which will be sent to all chambers of commerce in the UK, MPs, *The Times* Top 1,000 companies, the European Parliament, (the list goes on either until Uncle Tom Cobbleigh is mentioned, or you cough menacingly).'

'I'm certain you'll be interested in the chance to contribute editorial, supported by a full page advertisement, to the book, which incidentally has an introduction written by (prominent Cabinet minister or Captain of Industry).'

At this point, you interrupt to find out how much it costs. You're not quite sure how, but this question is side-stepped so that a few additional points can be made – perhaps some research quoted, publication date and deferred payment date stated, etc.

Finally, you will find that the package costs you either £2,995 or £3,500 and that an answer is needed by tomorrow.

If it is not needed by tomorrow, you will find that it is not needed for many months (with payment deferred still further). However, space 'is moving extremely fast' and 'we can only accept a maximum of x law firms/advertisers'.

Do not, on any account, believe the inference that time is of the essence. If it is, it probably means that they have failed to sell space or get organised and are now up against deadlines, in which case, stay clear. If the offer is so good that delay means someone else takes the space, live with the loss.

Nine times out of ten, or more, you will find that the opportunity remains viable for weeks or months. Whether it remains attractive depends on you determining the following:

- Does this conform to my advertising strategy? Does the publication promote an aspect of the practice that needs this form of boost?
- What circulation does it have? Is it paid for, or distributed free of charge?
- Is the publication the industry leader? If not, is it priced competitively?
- Can you have the facts faxed or posted to you, for consideration and internal circulation? (If not, don't touch it).
- Is this the first year of publication? If so, unfair as it may seem to what may be a prodigy in the making, you will probably be wise to

let the chance pass. If this is not the first year of publication, obtain a previous version. Does it look authoritative? Were your competitors in it?

- Can you see any press reviews of the directory?
- Do you have partner support for an entry, from the section of the firm which would be publicised through such advertising?
- Is your gut feeling in tune with what you have read and heard?
- Are your competitors going to be in the next edition? How and why?

Circulation – or readership?

Remember, circulation figures are fairly meaningless. If you are told that 30,000 copies are issued, ask if this means that 30,000 copies are individually requested. If the answer is yes, you will rarely put the phone down on anyone but an arrant liar.

Most of these general trade sector publications operate purely through advertising revenue, in the same way that a free newspaper functions. Thus the more that can be sent out, the better they look. It does not take a Machiavelli to realise the attraction of increasing the print run and sending out copies to an impressive list – whether they want it or not.

Though produced to high standards in many cases, often these directories are filed away on receipt without having the plastic wrapper unsealed. If you are told that copies are assiduously read and referred to by chief executives, ask to see the research to justify such a claim.

Don't be afraid of asking the salesperson for the names of a selection of recipients from previous years, whom you wish to call. If you do call such people, don't necessarily expect them to show great knowledge; if they simply know of the tome, consider appearing in it. If they don't, don't.

As a general rule, avoid this latter form of directory advertising unless you are absolutely sure it is a good idea. Pick all your directories only when you are happy that the sponsor or publisher is bona fide. Avoid fiddly small entries and concentrate on compiling impressive entries in known quantities.

IN SHORT

What is good advertising?

Bad advertising says what the firm wants to say, verbosely, irregularly and in the wrong publications.

Good advertising tells the client what he wants to know – or merely attracts his attention and hence interest. It does so consistently, in the publications the client reads.

It uses imagination instead of verbiage and it stands out from the crowd through its copy, layout and (when used) illustrative content.

Good advertising sells or implies benefits, not features and remains true to a single theme or service.

Summary

- Set an annual budget for advertising. If you cannot be exact, establish guidelines.
- Determine your market – the aspects of the firm which advertising should promote. This could be market sectors, the firm as a whole, or even individual transactions (if client permission is established).
- Check that the advertising follows the direction set by the marketing plan.
- Determine your message: what does the client want to hear? Use or conduct research as necessary.
- Determine the medium: where should you advertise? Decide between press and other forms of media. Gather media packs, ring contacts for their views. Research special features in publications, against which your message, if prominently displayed, might be particularly pertinent.
- Check on existing and future advertising costs, via BRAD (British Rates and Advertising Data). This directory carries details about publications, their circulation figures, rates and deadlines.
- Determine criteria by which opportunistic advertising opportunities should be accepted or turned down. You will receive regular calls offering space; it saves time to have a formula by which to respond.
- Decide whether to conduct a campaign, or to use advertising to support other initiatives. Don't advertise in isolation.
- Decide how you wish to advertise: by creating your own copy and having it set by magazines; by employing a designer to create

camera ready artwork configured to individual space bookings; or by employing an agency to handle all your advertising themselves.

- Keep records of all advertising bookings, with all deadlines marked. It is all too easy to miss a deadline or fail to chase a designer.
- Determine the total costs involved in booking space, using professional suppliers and producing camera ready artwork. Ensure this is in line with budgetary restrictions.
- Book space in your favoured publication(s).
- Draft copy for an advertisement. Make it interesting. Try to find a way to make your advertisement stand out from the crowd. Differentiate yourself.
- Commission any necessary illustrative material.
- Consider/add a response mechanism.
- Cut out all non-vital wording. Keep copy brief and headlines punchy. Allow illustrations or white space to dominate text.
- Check that all copy is client-oriented, not determined by what the firm wants to say.
- Have the advertisement set into camera ready artwork, to the dimensions of the space booked, and send it to the publication. Alternatively, send copy to the publication if they are to set it themselves. In the latter case, arrange to see and approve proofs.
- Ensure that copy, as it will appear, conforms to house style/corporate identity guidelines.
- Make sure that the firm and your clients know about the advertising. Remember that those who do not read a particular publication will not know about the prominence being accorded the firm. Consider whether to have a book in reception, carrying recent editorial references to, and articles about, the firm, along with recent advertising.

Directories

- Establish a policy on directories and stick to it: decide on criteria which determine whether entries are taken and in which media.
- Do not try to promote everything a firm does. Concentrate on strategically viable growth areas alone.
- Only take a directory entry if you are absolutely certain it is a good idea. If in doubt, stay out.

Hints and tips

- Negotiate with advertising representatives. There are always special placements or discounts to be had, if you are a regular advertiser.
- Book a series of placements, to qualify for discounts, to save administrative time and to cover several spots with one item of artwork.
- Always set yourself artificially early deadlines, thus building in a buffer zone against production problems, artwork going astray, or similar misadventures.
- Direct a lot of attention at small areas. Do not spread advertising thinly, where it will become invisible.
- Only appoint a specialist advertising agency if you have tens of thousands of pounds to allocate to this budget. Otherwise, do the job via a designer (and freelance copywriter if required).

4 Media relations

The Media. It sounds like a convention of spiritualists.

Tom Stoppard

To many lawyers, journalists seem as phantasmagorical as the above quote implies. As many myths exist about those who make their livings from newsprint as those who work in the law.

Some recurrent fallacies about the media:

1 'It's who you know, not what you know'

Knowing journalists can be a great help. Knowing who to go to when a story is there to be told can improve the chances of it finding a home. Having a friendly drink with a member of the press provides an opportunity to suggest and discuss ideas, or to build a relationship which allows you to explain the context of a story on a future occasion.

However, while there is value in this, it should not be overstated. Such wooing can be of much more use outside the professional services field. Publicity based on who you know often fails to pass the editor's spike. If there's no substance, there will be no story.

Your interest in dropping hints that will find their way into diary pieces is likely to be limited. There is little room for pure puffery in the publications you are likely to pursue.

Most of the time, you are likely to want to put your efforts into securing news or feature coverage which carries some weight. In this context, what you know is more important than who owes you a favour.

Your requirements are simple. An angle that will be of interest to a publication, and someone to make a decision on whether to accept or commission your contribution.

You do not need to have drunk wine bars dry with the editor of a publication to ring him up and discuss your idea.

Understandably, law firms are interested in gaining positive coverage. Most journalists are not in the least interested in helping to hype law firms. There are, of course, occasional exceptions. On occasion, a journalist will do a friend a favour and puff a firm. The story-seller will imply that part of his repertoire of attributes is having journalists in his pocket, thus perpetuating the myth that it is contacts alone that count in gaining coverage. The other 50 stories in that issue, resulting from hard work, written briefings, interviews and knowledgeable discussions, are conveniently ignored.

Anyone who relies on who they know to earn a living won't get far. It is a bonus, not an essential.

2 'All publicity is good publicity'

Whoever came up with this one never worked with a professional firm. If you are creating a splash around a film, book or record, notoriety is no bad thing. If you are selling contaminated mineral water or baby food, you might be able to gain plaudits from the way you cope with a crisis not entirely of your making. Even Hoover might claim to have their reputation and sales figures undented after their wrongheaded sales promotions went horribly wrong. But a professional firm succeeds or fails on the basis of its reputation. Its image needs to be nurtured and protected.

Therefore, all law firms need to strike a balance between seeking relationships with the media and safeguarding their reputation. The note of caution has to be offset by a readiness to communicate, but realistic measures must be taken to prevent – or at least contain – negative publicity. See Chapter 7 on Crisis Management.

3 'Most journalists are only interested in hatchet jobs'

Some, indeed, are interested in knocking copy. However, for every investigative or negative enquiry there are many opportunities to work alongside the press to mutual advantage. As Stephen Clues of Trowers & Hamlins observes, 'I believe the press should be accorded the same respect as a client. The relationship should be a mature one, based on respect for mutual professionals'.

If law firms cooperate with the media it often proves a help rather than a hindrance. Often, it is only when lawyers become suspicious or evasive that journalists pursue negative stories.

After centuries separated by publicity restrictions, lawyers have yet to accept fully the opportunities of working with the media. It is ironic that professions which both suffer from a mixed public perception should be divided by mutual suspicion.

There are many occasions when an editor needs to fill space with newsworthy stories and reliable background information. These are the occasions when lawyers and journalists can work together to mutual advantage. The former provides a service to the latter in terms of required material, the latter reciprocates with desired publicity.

A truth

When dealing with the press, television or radio, you pay nothing, and you relinquish control. You can take certain steps to control your message, but the final decisions are taken by editors. You have no right to approve copy or to reply. It is entirely at the discretion of the journalists involved whether and how they run stories. Unless you are libelled, you have no means of redress should coverage fail to appear as you would have wished.

It is important that law firms accept this as a fact of life. It is not a happy one, but it cannot be altered. Advertising is the only route for any firm which cannot live with the realities of media relations, for in advertising, you pay for the right to control your message which is then shaped purely to your specifications.

Fig 13

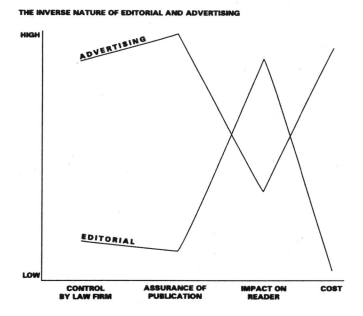

The importance of journalists

Gaining press coverage is not about single triumphs, nor is it about using the journalist simply as a conduit. Every article or item written gives you a chance to build your reputation with the journalist and the publication, these are targets in themselves. By building your profile with a journalist you can build your name in the market. The press are like bees, in that they carry and cross-pollenate ideas between otherwise static parties.

What to do when contacted by the media

It is important to welcome the approach. Before answering any questions, establish who you are talking to – the publication represented and the individual. Find out if this person is from advertising sales, or is an editorial contact. If the enquiry is general and uncontroversial, your willingness to cooperate should be manifest.

Obtain information on what the journalist actually requires. How many words, by when and in what format? Does he or she want quotes, and if so, to whom should they be attributed? Is any supporting material needed, such as photographs or diagrams?

If your response is straightforward (corroboration of a fact, for example), write it down as you speak, then fax it through to the journalist as confirmation. If the enquiry demands a considered response, or you are asked for a quote on an issue, ask for the caller's deadline. Fax through a reply as far in advance of this as you can.

If the enquiry is controversial, or you do not know the answer, do not, under any circumstances, guess or give a flippant reply. Remaining polite and helpful, ascertain exactly what is required and by when, then inform the journalist that you or a colleague will respond.

Even if you cannot then frame a suitable response, make sure that you explain this. As well as being a courtesy that will help maintain friendly relations with the publication in question, this should preclude the appearance of a snide 'so and so refused to comment'.

What should you say?

If you have something to say, either unilaterally or in response to an enquiry, consider whether it is of interest. As marketeer Kim Tasso advises 'like any other aspect of marketing, you must adopt the point of view of your target audience. This means you have to try to think like a journalist. You have to translate your information into a form that is of interest and relevance to the individual journalist and his or her readers. This is the art of identifying an "angle" '. Always put your story into context, so that misrepresentations have less likelihood of creeping into print.

When to issue a press release

What is news? The cliché that 'dog bites man' is not, but that 'man bites dog' is, may be accurate in terms of the popular press, but doesn't help much when it comes to publicising a law firm.

Every development within the firm is news. The determinant as to whether it merits an attempt at wider publicity, therefore, lies partly in the question 'is this of interest to anyone?', and (more importantly) in asking 'if this were to appear in the press, would my clients be interested?' Most importantly, are you confident that the news will reflect positively on you?

If the answers to these questions are in the affirmative, if the story can be framed so as to appear interesting, and if it will comply with the publicity code, then there is a case for gathering information together.

The most likely vehicle for this information is a press release.

How to write a press release

Every book ever written on media relations dictates the basic rules of press release writing – yet the consensus suggests that up to 96% of all press releases are binned on arrival. What is going wrong?

The reasons are many. Naturally, there is not room for everyone's publicity material to find its way into print. Most editors arrive in their offices to be met by mountains of press releases. Purely on the basis of available space, most have no chance of receiving a typesetter's attentions.

However, the truth is that most press releases are poorly written. It would appear that prescriptions for press release production are still falling on deaf ears and closed eyes.

As guilty as the writer may be, often it is the partnership who must bear the blame for unpublishable material. A release written by a committee will often tear the heart out of a story, leaving an obscure assembly of facts. If it is too hard to understand at a glance, it won't see the light of day. Equally, solid news has to say something. An over-cautious editing process often leads to a firework display being reduced to a squib.

Conversely, an over-eager writer may try to pass off a squib as a firework display!

The essential point in press release writing is to convey the story immediately. The opening headline should grab attention. You then have only the first two lines of the copy to fix that attention. While the rest of the copy should be concise and well-crafted, you can relax to some extent. If they read this the journalist has probably already been hooked.

That vital first paragraph needs to answer – succinctly and without hype – the questions Who?, What? and When? Paragraph two can then deal with Why? and How? Remember this rule alone, and you are most of the way there.

The rest of the release can then be devoted to additional pertinent detail and perhaps a quote or two. The quotes are almost always a waste of time and space, since they rarely add anything to the story. Most are along the lines of 'Bloggins welcomed the appointment, saying that it signalled a tremendous opportunity for Tripley, Hall and Gaunt.' Editors do run this waffle from time to time, but only when being lazy or when unaccountably short of space-fillers.

The rule with quotes, given on paper or verbally, is to make them pithy. A short succinct statement may find itself into a headline. It is likely to be reproduced in the text. A ramble, with subclauses, will not find its way into print at all.

Many people feel that they have only earned their pay if they can stretch two paragraphs of detail into four pages of padding. This should be a shooting offence. Faced with a rainforest of paper every morning, the first thing most editors do is glance through the press releases to see what can be filed under 'bin'. Since there is more satisfaction to be had in getting rid of a bulky document than a single page, the over-long release is more likely to get short shrift than the pithy version.

But what if you have a lot of salient information to convey?

Save it. If it can't be conveyed on two pages (and preferably one), allude to the additional information. You will be contacted for further information should the story merit it. Make sure that you provide adequate points of contact and telephone numbers (including home if appropriate) so that these additional questions can be fielded. If you are not contacted, the journalist received what was needed to fill the space available.

In the (unusual) few cases where additional points just have to be conveyed, send them as ancillary notes to the press release. Remember, when faced by hundreds of competing sheets of paper, the reader needs your help in providing easy access to your news.

Alternatives to the press release

Because journalists receive so many press releases, an alternative format or vehicle may increase your publicity's chance of being noticed and thus used.

Consider the creative presentation of your story. Perhaps issuing original research, a survey, or even a 'trend watch' may be more effective than just another press release. The latter might identify a perceived trend in the legal marketplace, or a market sector. You can then hope to be rewarded through coverage which notes your having spotted the trend. Your press material should have added commentary on the impact this trend is having, and outlined what your firm is going to do about this. Both these observations should lead to additional references in any resulting material.

Similarly, you may wish to consider issuing fact sheets on topical issues – brief newsletters aimed solely or primarily at the media. Press briefings of this sort, including newsworthy commentary from the partnership, will often be regurgitated as the views of the journalist, but more often will result in attribution. The way such stories appear tends to lend greater editorial endorsement than simple reproduction of press information in a news story.

Use existing stories

It is not always necessary to spend time thinking up ways of 'placing' stories. Why create news when it already exists? Before dreaming up a series of new initiatives, think about what is happening within the firm that can be publicised.

This may mean building a news angle into a forthcoming seminar. For the latter to be successful, it must have a topical angle. Think about whether this contains a news story or a feature idea.

If you are involved in developing new services, your marketing efforts may be directed to market research. If this is the case, can the results of the research be published? You will not wish to divulge sensitive findings, but may have a lot to gain from publicising your newfound understanding of a market and thus demonstrating both your knowledge and foresight.

If you are conducting research that has no conceivable media angle, consider adding a few questions designed to elicit news stories. Ask a few controversial questions, gauge responses to topical issues. Then release the results of this section of the research to the press.

Who should be on your mailing list?

Ideally, you should not have a mailing list. Far better is a media database, listing editorial staff and specialist correspondents. This database would indicate the broad interests of each publication and the regular features which are open to editorial contributions.

Commercial organisations offer access to such databases, but are unlikely to prove cost-effective unless you issue regular press releases to vast numbers of the media.

However, in most cases a mailing list suffices and functions adequately. It is often compiled from addresses gleaned from back copies of magazines, media directories and packs of sales information sent to you by hungry advertising departments.

Every press release needs a bespoke mailing list. There is no point sending fabulous news about your commercial joint venture work to *Estates Weekly*. All that does is cause *Estates Weekly* to look upon your next commercial property announcement with a jaundiced eye. If you are going to the trouble of issuing information, make sure you have a comprehensive list of publications on your list, whittled down as appropriate to each release. With each release, only those who have some chance of reproducing the story should be left on the list.

This is modishly known as 'targeting' – the antithesis of the so-called 'scattergun' approach, where you send everything to everyone in the hope that some of your seed will escape stony ground.

A word of warning. Don't get too puritanical about your targeting. Being over cautious is as bad as being over liberal in your distribution. For the cost of an extra stamp and sheet of paper, try the longshots as well as the racing certainties. The only caveat, therefore, is to make sure that the target publication covers the area pertinent to your publicity, ie that there is some hope of coverage, rather than just wasting a hard-pressed editor's time.

There are a lot of purists who dictate that you should be able to guarantee interest from a publication before you sully their offices with your press release. Public relations professionals, who have been scattering bits of paper for years, tend to look askance at these 'untargeted' mailings. However, all will have had the experience of a low-hope release generating useful coverage in an unexpected quarter.

Amazingly enough, editors have been known to show lateral thinking in their selection of what to publish.

Use a directory, such as those published by Two Ten or PIMS, to select the appropriate media and correspondent for your information. BRAD, Willings or Benns directories will give you useful information about publications and their circulations, but are less useful when it comes to named correspondents.

Target readers, not magazines

Remember that the recipient for any release should be that publication read by actual and potential clients. Thus if you are an environmental lawyer, your target is the trade press writing about environmental issues. Journals covering your specialisation are known as your 'vertical' press, whereas legal publications are considered 'horizontal'. You need to be in the vertical press far more than you should be pursuing the legal press. The latter may enhance your reputation in your field, but the former is usually where the new business lies.

Supporting the press release

A favourite waste of time in media relations work is to spend hours on the phone checking on the right correspondent to receive your bumf. Journalists on larger publications, naturally unaware if your story is a candidate for the spike or the front page, will wearily direct you to the first name that comes into their heads.

Smaller publications revolve around decisions made by the editor, news editor and features editor. Your directory has probably got their names wrong, since journalists move from publication to publication with surprising regularity.

Therefore, send news stories to the news editor (personalised only if you are certain of his or her name), features to the features editor (ditto) and Letters to the Editor to – the editor. This revolutionary system increases the likelihood of your story being picked up.

By now, seasoned professionals will be in a ferment over the above. Quite right too. For they will have noted that these words of wisdom do not apply to the truly scintillating story.

Selling in a big story

For a development of definite consequence, the danger is that your gem will disappear under the mountains of waffle on the journalist's desk. In this case, the suggestions above are largely redundant.

MEDIA RELATIONS

The major event press release should be written in the same way, but needs to be pre-sold and followed up. If you have a significant announcement to make, you will need to list your media contacts in order of importance.

Telephone in advance, to forewarn each journalist that your story is en route. Pass on enough details to whet the appetite, but not enough to relay the entire story – unless, of course, you want to risk the unauthorised version finding its way into print. It may be wise simply to read the first paragraph of the press release to your contact.

Personal communication with each correspondent, promising written information by fax to follow, should be enough to convey your excitement. Once you have enthused sufficiently to elicit definite interest, find out whether your contact will be in the office to receive the information when released. If not, to whom should the information be directed, and should it be sent by post or fax.

A follow-up call to check that the release has been received gives you the opportunity to gauge whether the story is likely to run. However, please note: it is usually a waste of time to follow up inconsequential stories.

Journalists abhor the 'did you get my release about so and so' call. Unless you have a genuinely good story which a journalist would hate to miss, or a second reason for the call – a new angle or story – you are merely going to lose credit and credibility.

More often than not in a big story, you are going to want to maximise publicity, control its timing and ensure that your most important press contacts are able to run the piece within their issue deadlines.

Obviously, therefore, you need to know these deadlines. There is no point in issuing a story by fax on Wednesday meant for *Corporate World* whose weekly deadline is Tuesday. Their less important competitor, *Business Europe*, whose deadline is Thursday, then picks up the story to the chagrin of both you and *Corporate World*.

The solution in a case such as this is to pre-issue *Corporate World* with the story, under embargo. An embargo states the earliest time when information can be released. Embargoed to Wednesday, your story is safe with *Corporate World*, which will not appear in print until Thursday. Such planning ensures that both publications are given the opportunity of publishing your news.

If *Corporate World* is sufficiently important to you, you may prefer to negotiate an exclusive, thereby improving the likelihood of your story being carried. However, this falls into the category of putting all your eggs into one basket. Unless you are looking at a sector which has only

66

one strong publication and many weak ones, exclusives are probably best avoided.

One to one briefings

If you decide to release a major story, the best way of ensuring that the most important media get full and accurate details is to invite them, in advance, to meet your spokesman for a briefing.

Ideally, you should book that spokesman for a full day. Telephone the journalists in person, revealing enough of the story to engender interest. Ask them whether they would be free to attend a one-to-one briefing on the specified date. If necessary, fax through a short précis of the facts, making it clear that the story is embargoed (cannot be run) until your favoured time and date. This process should be enough to convey the import and impact of the development.

Make sure your contacts pencil into their diaries an agreed time, which you can then confirm in writing. If the day proves inconvenient, and no deputy can be sent, try to arrange a briefing in advance, stressing again the strict embargo on the release of information. This approach should also be taken when you know that a publication's copy and press dates require that advance notification of news be given.

Schedule briefings at hourly intervals. It is advisable, though not essential, to try to avoid departing journalists seeing new arrivals.

A briefing needs to be both high level and comprehensive. If you invite the senior reporters or editors of publications to attend a personal briefing, they will expect the senior or managing partner to be present. Don't fob them off with waffle, with a junior partner uncertain of the press, or with a marketing representative.

However, make sure that a marketeer is present. This person's role is to record information disseminated at the meeting, provide follow-up material to the journalist, to contribute where necessary (though such contributions should be kept to the minimum) and to learn.

Such involvement should never constitute the mouthpiece of the organisation. This makes the partner look like a puppet and irritates the journalist, who will only prefer to attribute quotes to a marketing professional when covering a purely marketing angle.

Interviews in general

When being interviewed, at a briefing, over the phone or even over lunch, remain on your guard. Remember, anything you say may be taken down and used. Anything you say may be turned around and misused, so be careful not to accept leading statements by a journalist, or to remain ambiguous on a subject. Think before you respond.

Some journalists believe 'off the record' means something. Others do not. So the simplest course is to assume that anything you say may be reproduced in print. If you want something kept quiet, keep quiet.

Prepare in advance the things you want to say. Put over two or three key points you would like to have published. Repeat them. Put your points forcefully and avoid mentioning any negatives or criticising any third parties.

Convey your story, then change the subject (if the meeting is informal). Ask if there are other subjects relating to the firm which are of interest, then terminate the discussion.

Ask the journalist to let you know when a piece might appear and make it clear that you are happy to be called for any facts to be checked or additional points to be made.

Treat a meeting with a journalist as you would any other business meeting. Set an agenda, prepare supporting material and follow up with a note of the meeting.

What is a press conference?

Usually it is a waste of time and money. In certain circumstances it can save both.

In the days when PR professionals knew every journalist, 'placed' stories over G&Ts and ran up enormous lunch bills, the press conference evolved as the complementary approach to the 'one-to-one briefing'.

The idea was that, with a story of any magnitude, it would be more effective to gather the press together and impress them with an announcement. Adding visual bangs and whistles was deemed a sure-fire way to impress the journalists. Videos were shot, displays mounted and expensive caterers hired.

The intention was to persuade media guests to cover the story behind the glitz. Fuelled by liberal quantities of booze and an exotic lunch, the grateful hack would wax lyrical.

And it worked.

And it still works. Very occasionally. Expensively.

The day of the press conference has passed. The budgets are not available for the lavish events, and even the basic event is out of favour. The main reason is that journalists are too pressed for time.

A long lunch hour is a luxury few can afford. Additionally, attending an event with the competition prevents a new or exclusive angle being found. Therefore, most journalists prefer personal interviews – ie one to one briefings.

When to hold a press conference

The case for press conferences rests on three main grounds. The first is the immediacy and impact that such a gathering creates. Calling a conference adds weight. The second is justification on the grounds of sheer importance – when you find yourself in a 'seller's market' with regard to information. If you know that your news is certain to be of general interest, a conference allows you to shape and control its announcement.

The third reason for holding a press conference is connected to the second: urgency. If something needs to be made public quickly, calling a press conference serves as a public invitation to share in the announcement. In the event of a major crisis, it is good public relations to hold a press conference.

How to hold a press conference

Organising such an event is a hair-raising business. No one is ever sure who will come. If you hire a room for 100, five may turn up. Arrange to invite a select group, and, mysteriously, the word may spread and twice the room capacity may turn up (a preferable problem, but a problem nonetheless).

If possible, book a room that can be partitioned or partially screened off. This will give you the flexibility to expand the auditorium if numbers so demand, while averting the threat of eerie expanses between journalists, should numbers be few.

Make sure you book enough time for rehearsals. Prepare a list of questions that might be asked, so that your speaker(s) can prepare adequate responses.

Recruit enough people to help out by meeting and greeting, recording the names and publications of the press and helping out generally. Make sure these people know enough about why the conference is being held so that they do not react idiotically to media questions, but are briefed against producing anything bar the party line when it comes to being drawn out by the press. This is the time for them to stress the firm's track record and strengths.

Visit the venue in advance with the checklist that ends this book's chapter on seminars. Do not leave until you are satisfied that the staff at the venue can answer all your queries adequately.

Make a nuisance of yourself. Test the audio visual equipment. Draw the curtains to ensure that the room can be adequately blacked out. Ask about what events are happening at the same time as yours and how much noise can be anticipated. Find out where the lavatories are, where cars can be parked and coats hung.

Taste the house wine and ask to meet the person who will be on duty at the time of the event. Check that the signage will be adequately visible and that the records spell the firm's name correctly. Establish what will happen if 50 people all arrive at exactly the same moment.

Prepare an area for photography, making sure that it is adequately supplied by power points. In some cases it may be appropriate to ensure that there is a prominent logo visible in the background, should photographs be taken in this spot. Such 'placement' is standard for many commercial organisations launching products or services, but may only be relevant in limited cases for law firms, who are more likely to call large press conferences only when crises hit home.

Having covered all the points on your checklist, walk through the entire progression from arrival to event to departure, to confirm that you are fully au fait with equipment, locations and procedures.

Press pack

However many facts you impart orally, and however much the journalist may scribble, the core of any major story is found in the press pack. This will normally comprise a main press release and an indeterminate amount of 'background'. If there are more than two documents, it is usual to present this information in a press folder.

One common sin is to fill this folder with tracts of information, when most if not all journalists want to get to the bare bones of the story. It is preferable to keep information short and to the point, while compiling and holding in reserve the more arcane or detailed background, to be used as supplementary information. Any journalist who decides to cover the story in-depth will make contact for additional information.

This omission of extraneous material therefore serves to improve the chances of the press accurately covering the basics of your story; it means that anyone looking for detail makes contact, allowing you to track response and possibly intercept misconceptions or problems; and it saves forests.

Another *faux pas* is the production of ornate press folders, stuffed with overdesigned, mastheaded press release paper. Simple, professional presentation should be the rule, not ornate frippery. The media are not impressed by production values, but by the clear presentation of a story.

Get this right, and your reward will be an accurate story, often utilising the wording of the press pack material. Get it wrong, and you risk a damaging, inaccurate report of proceedings.

Photography

An enormous amount of money is spent arranging photography for magazines which don't want it. However, since a photographer's day or half-day rate is unchanged, however many prints you need, you may incur up to 95% of the cost before producing a single photograph. Therefore, it is not as wasteful as it seems to order relatively inexpensive prints to be sent out willy nilly (although it is fairly ridiculous if the publication doesn't use photography).

Order 7 by 5 inch black and white images. Type out a caption, describing the person or situation depicted, ensuring that your firm's name is given, and adding your name and number for further information. This should be glued to the back of the photograph. On no account write directly onto the reverse of the photograph, as this will create an impression on the front.

Firms should ensure that they keep an up-to-date picture library, including photographs of all partners.

Picture story

A picture story is merely an extended photocaption (or abbreviated press release) attached to a photograph. If you have got a story which is best explained in a picture, issue it as a picture story. Don't waste your creativity and time trying to explain what is obvious from the image.

Although it should be avoided, if you feel the need to attach the photograph to the press release with a paper clip, make sure that the image is face down and your clip is affixed over an unimportant part of the photo. The clip's impression is bound to transfer to the image.

How to sell in a feature idea

If 'man bites dog/lawyer offers new service' is news, then 'why man bit dog/why lawyer is offering new service' is a feature. News is immediate. It makes announcements. Features explore issues.

The news pages on publications are oversupplied and often difficult to penetrate, In many cases, the feature which provides the heart of the magazine are accorded less attention by firms and their publicists. This presents an opportunity to the astute marketeer.

Let us assume that your firm does a lot of work in the banking sector. If you are monitoring the progress of forthcoming legislation, or are considering how a previous Act of Parliament will affect topical banking developments, then you may have views of interest to the financial marketplace in general.

It is often worth investigating whether key publications in the relevant market have editorial features planned within which you might make a contribution. Partners and fee earners can then tailor their synopsised ideas to such a feature. However, many publications will run an article on a stand-alone basis, that is, if you make a good case for doing so in your synopsis (particularly if you can make a case for topicality). The synopsis serves three purposes.

- It will crystallise your information.
- It will act as your briefing sheet when you ring a features editor on an appropriate publication. You will only have one chance to put across your idea – the synopsis should help you do so succinctly.
- Most importantly, once the journalist has expressed interest, the synopsis can be sent to the publication. This ensures that, when you are contacted (or re-establish contact yourself) to be given a commission to write an article, both you and the journalist are in complete agreement over what should be covered.

The alternative may be being asked to write on a subject, putting hours into drafting a feature, and then being told that the article isn't exactly what the feature editor wanted.

The synopsis should begin, like a press release, with a headline that encompasses the material. A single sentence should then describe each of the following:

- Purpose of the article.
- To whom it will be of interest.
- Topicality.

The rest of the synopsis should be restricted to the same page, giving a précis of the key points to be covered in the proposed article. These should be numbered and consist of no more than seven or eight points.

Once asked to write, how do you go about creating readable copy? For the lawyer, this may sound insulting, but the truth is that few lawyers write easily. As Martin Edwards, a partner of Mace & Jones explains, 'solicitors are supposed to be good with words, yet a skillful advocate is not necessarily competent to write interestingly'.

However excellent your grammar and command of language, all legal training directs you to a degree of accuracy that would seem pedantic in most articles. Writing for the media is utterly different from drafting legal documentation. Rather than seeking comprehensivity, you need to favour comprehensibility.

If called upon to write a feature, start by noting down what it is you are trying to achieve. Think about this from the viewpoint of the reader of the publication for which you are writing. Who are you writing for? What will they find interesting? How technical is the publication and how much detail can you/should you cover in the space available?

Aim for clarity throughout. Avoid the length of sentence which is standard in legal documentation. In fact, aim for the shortest, pithiest sentences you can bear.

This does not mean strip away all decoration. Use the optional extras of language, not just the prosaic core. Throw in idioms, anecdotes, metaphors and similes to heighten readability.

Appeal directly to the reader. Use the active rather than the passive. Rather than refer to how one might be affected by new legislation, frame an example and explain how the reader is affected by hypothetical developments you introduce into your narrative. You may wish to use the device of writing in an artificial present tense, rather than merely report.

You have just read the paragraphs above. Do they persuade? Do they tell you anything new? Do they engage your attention and demand agreement or refutation?

If the answer is 'yes' to all these questions, the writing is alive. Bring your articles to life.

Editing

The comments above apply as much, if not more, to the article's editor. This person will probably be a marketing professional and thus constitutionally more likely to accept the reasons for such an approach.

Thus if you find yourself editing turgid material, inject life and reconfigure the text so that it looks less like a complex bit of book learning and more like an informative and, dare we hope, entertaining read. As Stephen Clues of Trowers & Hamlins observes, one of the most damaging things you can do in media relations is work hard to obtain a commission and then submit it late and either too long or too short. These are mistakes made time and again with the press. In my view, they are almost unforgiveable.

With this in mind, ensure that you establish the word count required by the publication. Use the word count facility on your/your secretary's word processor to check that you have not exceeded the total. If you have, it is preferable that you, rather than the publication, edit to size.

Find out if photography is needed. If so, what can you offer, and what does the publication suggest? Is the requirement for colour transparencies or black and white prints?

What is the deadline? Most publications will give you a little leeway on this, but never assume that this will be so. If you are relaying the deadline to a colleague, who is writing the article, give him or her an artificially tight deadline. It is far better – though unusual – to be two weeks early with copy than half a day late. Aim for two weeks early and, allowing for vital work, holidays, the search for corroboration of an elusive fact, and the more usual 'I'm so sorry, I completely forgot', you should have a fair chance of meeting deadlines.

Advertorials

Editorial gains its value from objectivity. Be wary of 'opportunities' put your way by publications, which link editorial to advertising (see similar advice under the directories section of the chapter on advertising). Such options entail either your editorial being dependant on buying supporting advertising space, or looking like editorial but requiring you to purchase the space. The latter copy will appear with the word 'advertorial' or 'advertisement feature' written above it.

It would be wrong to write off all such ventures as tawdry. While most should be regarded with suspicion, there may be value in testing the water. Nonetheless, this is not a recommended option for most firms, in that the publication is unlikely to have authority and true profile and the advertorial vehicle is likely to undermine editorial impact.

Using published material

If you are lucky enough to have your efforts blessed with publication, do not let the fruits of your labours go unseen. Arrange to have articles reprinted, so that high quality copies can be used in publicity ventures. The publisher can usually arrange such reprints more cheaply than your own printer, particularly if you know in advance that the article is being run. In such cases, you may be able to request special 'run-ons', added at the time of the original printing, solely for your benefit.

When reprinting, make sure that text is overprinted with the firm's logo and address. Some commentators recommend having the date dropped from such reprints, so as to allow long-term use. Whether or not this course is taken depends on whether the copy has in-built longevity. If it does not, leave the date, since its omission may imply that the article is no longer topical.

These reprints can be added to press packs and used on exhibition stands and at seminars. Copies can be mailed to clients, 'for information' or with a covering letter drawing attention to any particularly interesting or topical points made.

Additionally, press cuttings or reprints can be displayed in reception areas. In exceptional cases, it may be worth having authoritative and positive coverage blown up and framed, for display within the firm.

Make sure that references to the firm in the news are reported internally, through bulletin boards, the in-house newsletter, and, in cases of major stories, through internal memoranda forewarning staff of the coverage or drawing their attention to major developments.

Whichever course is taken, the lesson with regard to media coverage remains the same: recycle it.

MEDIA RELATIONS

Summary

Dealing with the media in general

- Favour researching factual information over lunching journalists.
- Anticipate and plan refutation of negative interpretations, prior to releasing positive-seeming stories.
- Treat the press with cautious respect, not as salivating jackals.
- Control what goes out from the firm, but never expect to control what is published.
- Keep notes of what was said to whom. Follow up telephone conversations with written confirmation.
- If you do not know an answer, note the question, but don't guess at a response. Promise a reply once you have investigated further. Ensure you keep your promise.
- Think from the point of view of the reader and journalist, in shaping replies to enquiries.

Press announcements

- Only issue press release information if it qualifies as genuine news, will reflect positively (or limit damage), complies with the Law Society Publicity Code and will impress/inform clients.
- Keep press releases short, factual and immediately comprehensible.
- Cover the who, what and when in the first paragraph.
- Leave the how and why to paragraph two.
- Keep quotes succinct.
- Relegate all background material to ancillary notes. Ideally, retain these against the possibility of future enquiries, rather than issue them. If you must issue them, highlight the fact that they are supplementary notes to the main (maximum two, preferably one) page story.
- Consider packaging your material in a fashion more interesting to the media than a press release. Differentiate to stand out.
- Investigate and use existing stories rather than create new 'angles' from a vacuum.
- Build bespoke mailings, based on the nature of the story.
- Use the telephone to support important stories, but never to check receipt of less vital information.
- Set up and hold one-to-one briefings if a story is of major importance.

76

- Plan ahead for briefings and announcements to accommodate deadlines of key publications. Stress embargoes where necessary.
- Rehearse and record briefing content. Avoid 'off the record' pronouncements.
- Hold press conferences only when you have a story of guaranteed interest to the public in general, where complete control of an urgent announcement is imperative, and where it is vital that the announcement is seen to be public.
- Plan press conferences using the checklist at the end of this book's section on seminars.
- Stage a rehearsal, with awkward questions thrown and fielded.
- Compile a press pack, based on pertinent information, not design values.
- Produce photography only when target publications are known to run images. Produce colour pictures only if a publication does not use black and white.
- The usual format is 7' x 5' black and white. Glue descriptive details and your name/contact details to the reverse.
- If the picture tells your story, affix brief details to the reverse (making it a 'picture story') rather than add superfluous information through a separate press release.

Placing a feature

- Determine who you want to read the article.
- Establish which publication(s) is/are read by such people.
- Ring the favoured publications' advertising departments for a forward feature list and a copy of the publication.
- Agree a working title for the article.
- Synopsise topical/main interest angles into one sentence.
- Add up to eight bullet points detailing key points that would be made by the article.
- Call the editorial departments of the appropriate publications, in the order of suitability to your goals/article. Find out which editor, journalist or section should be approached with the article idea.
- 'Sell in' the suggestion that your firm contribute the article. Major on the relevance and topicality to the publication's readers. Offer to send the synopsis.
- If the idea is rejected and the journalist is not peremptory, ask if there are other subjects or opportunities for a legal contribution.
- If the idea is accepted, establish what is to be covered, the word-count required, and the deadline.

- Produce/adapt your one page synopsis, in bullet points. This ensures neither writer nor editor misunderstands what is required.
- Give whoever will be writing the article a false (early) deadline. Treat this as sacrosanct unless absolutely necessary.
- Find out if photography or other illustrative material is wanted. Check if copy is needed on disk, or as 'hard copy' (ie printed out).
- Check on, and chase, copy. The earlier you get it, the more time you will have to edit.
- Try to build a mention of the firm's name into the text – but not more than once.
- Ensure that the article is bylined by name, title and the firm's name.
- Send the copy with your with contact details (name and telephone number), in case of queries.
- Telephone to establish receipt of the article, satisfaction with the copy, and the anticipated publication date.
- Ask if a follow-up article would be welcome, on a similar or associated subject.
- Consider whether offprints – printed copies of the article alone – would be useful for publicity purposes. Arrange this through your contact well in advance of the publication date.
- Use the opportunity afforded by a successfully placed article to get to know the journalist and his/her interests.

Hints and tips

- Because most journalists in the national press work late, they start late. They often attend lunchtime briefings or events, and face their busiest time in the late afternoons (deadlines). Therefore, your best chance of winning attention and selling your information lies between 10.30am and 12.30pm. You may have to rely on the 3pm to 4pm spot as a back-up.
- Find out when your key publications' press days are (the day on which copy is printed). This is a busy day and should be avoided unless you have a burning, time-sensitive story to release.
- When suggesting a feature idea, it is polite – and often appreciated – to ask whether you are calling at a good or bad time. If it is the latter, ask when would be a good time to call back. The temptation to dump your story regardless is counterproductive; not only will your seed fall on stony ground, but you will lose goodwill.
- Put yourself in the journalist or reader's position. Is there a story? What is the angle that would interest you if you were a reader of the publication?

- Write down the key words or phrases that will help you to 'sell' your idea. You need to convey its essence and attractions succinctly and swiftly.
- Contact the most influential publications in the sectors you are targeting. Ask the advertising department for media packs, with forward feature lists. This should give you several months' notice of when your specialisations will be covered. There is then an opportunity to suggest appropriate contributions.
- Subscribe to a media directory. These will give you most, if not all, of the contact names, addresses and telephone numbers you need.
- Include the media in your new publication and newsletter mailings, and in seminar invitations.
- Tape record interviews, particularly sensitive ones. Do this openly, not surreptitiously.
- Whatever your subject, plan in advance, write out and then work in positive allusions to the practice. Sell in up to three key strengths in this way.
- Never follow up a press release to ask why the story did not get more/better coverage.

5 Publications

In the days of 1980s confusion, the professions edged suspiciously into self-promotion by producing a brochure. Then they stopped, looked at the end result, questioned the cost, and stacked the brochures in reception and on storage shelves. When asked about marketing, they stated that they had tried it and found it sadly lacking.

A caricature to be sure, but there are still first cousins to those who practised such an approach. In addition, there is a school of thought which, based on a more balanced assessment, agrees that publications are not worth the paper they are printed on.

Yet most professional firms produce brochures and consider them an integral part of their promotional efforts. Where lies the truth?

As always, the answer is that it lies somewhere between these two extremes. Publications have an important role to play in promoting a firm – but they are close to useless when produced to stand alone.

What is a publication?

For the sake of this book and chapter, a publication is defined as a document produced by the firm for promotional purposes. The most obvious example is the corporate brochure (the term 'corporate' is used laxly here to include a firm or partnership).

One reason why the corporate brochure has become a rather maligned beast in recent years is boredom. The first professional brochures minted or borrowed copy and shone with the novelty of images. Yet ennui has begun to set in. 'Brochure-speak' is a term of derision, directed at hyperbole and stock phrases. Brochures are seen by some as vehicles for the corporate puff, unreadable and expensive to produce.

So why do firms feel that they must have one? An oft-given reason is that clients expect it. It is a brave organisation that can reach a certain size and do without.

There is more to the brochure, however, than this negativity would imply. A well written example does more than tub thump. It can provide concise information, create an impression, and act as an important element in a mix of promotional tools and activities designed to impress and create impact.

If sufficient care is put into its creation, a corporate brochure can often help refine as well as reflect a firm's structure and strengths. It coalesces the entire range of an organisation's skills and markets served. Laid out properly, it communicates what the firm can do for the reader, in terms that convey a practical benefit.

Far from being important, a brochure is often essential in providing a quick picture of an organisation.

Form and content

A firm's brochure is often called upon to act as a microcosm of the firm itself. It should mirror the qualities for which the firm is, and wants to be, known. In many ways, therefore, form is more important than content.

We judge books by their covers. A brochure needs to lend impact, to look good, and to match the identity of its progenitor. As with giving a presentation, while the content is indubitably important, the essential effect is created by the way in which the information is conveyed. Design, print and materials are usually more important than text.

If corporate brochures had to earn their budget through being read, they might be an endangered species. In fact, many brochures are never read. The impression they make is conveyed through their look, feel and layout, gauged during a quick thumbing-through.

The publications range

Publications fall into two main groups: the overtly promotional (brochures) and the subtly promotional (newsletters, guides and similar informative productions).

Alongside the corporate brochure, an organisation may choose to promote products, services or market expertise through ancillary brochures. Many will then look at publishing options which demonstrate their expertise in a given sector.

Informative publications, such as sector updates or research reports, are more targeted than brochures. They usually deal with issues which are attracting the attention of potential and actual clients in a given sector of the market. Distributed correctly, such publications can be very effective, insinuating a selling message into a package that is of immediate use to a genuinely interested reader.

Newsletters aimed at the outside world fall somewhere in the middle. Many are self-indulgent and focused on the firm's activities (rather than why the reader should be interested in such activities).

The better examples, however, provide highly topical news and analysis, served up in regular instalments. Here, the brochure formula is reversed. Presentation and general appearance is secondary; what matters most is content.

Publication essentials

Ideally, all publications should stem from a consistent corporate identity (see Chapter 2). Specifications should be set in stone, in a corporate identity manual.

In reality, many firms agree and fix such an identity after an evolutionary process, rather than as a first step. Publications arise in a vacuum.

Assuming this to be the case, it is essential to impose some initial shape on all publications. Where more than one document appears, all should look related.

This means that the firm's name should use the same typography, with the same height, dimensions and position on the page in each manifestation.

It is well worth asking a designer to provide you with 'bromides' (forms of camera-ready artwork) of your firm's name or logo. These can then be sent to any typesetter or printer, to establish conformity in the way your name appears. Even if other elements vary, at least the most important should look right. If you fail to do this, you risk a plethora of different styles appearing – or even misspellings.

Just as every effort should be made to make visual images consistent, the same attention should be paid to print materials and quality.

Why?

One reason why publications are important to the professions lies in the nature of work conducted. Most of it is invisible. Much of it is displayed as sheets of white paper since service organisations, lawyers, accountants, surveyors et al have very little to physically demonstrate the service on offer. Without products to show, an attractive publication goes a long way. That is why it is so important to not only get each publication right, but to ensure that, displayed together, they demonstrate a firm in control. As with all aspects of controlling a corporate identity, consistency of production conveys good planning and organisational skills.

What does it cost?

Like so many promotional activities, there are few obvious rules of thumb to determine what publications cost. The variables are many, including quality of materials, colour used, amount of alterations required to typesetting and proofs, number of copies printed and cost of new artwork produced.

In her book *Marketing and Communications Techniques for Architects*, Lynne Choona Ryness opines that 'the average cost of producing a 16 page, full-colour brochure is somewhere between £15,000 and £30,000'. However, a similar job could probably be done for between £5,000 and £10,000 if certain circumstances were engineered. These might include using standard colours and paper stocks, reproducing existing photography or images, finalising text prior to setting, reducing print runs (see below) and pauperising your suppliers.

'But,' you may interject at this point, 'you can produce brochures for hundreds, not thousands of pounds.' Indeed you can. You can even print thousands of cheap one colour fliers for tens rather than hundreds of pounds. The key variable is quality, and its main determinants are the nature of paper and the amount of colour you want to use.

An indication of the effect colour can have on price is given below.

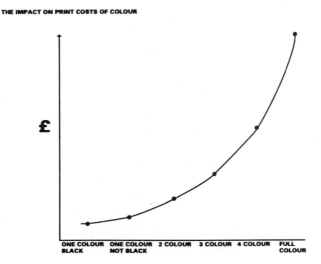

Fig 14

Getting started on a corporate brochure

Almost certainly, the first brochure produced by a firm is the one which reflects the entire entity, not just an aspect of the service provided. This 'corporate' brochure will become the touchstone, determining how future publications should look.

As the most obvious manifestation of a firm, it is going to be of considerable interest to the firm's partners and staff. The former in particular will have strong views on how it should look. Do you consult or impose?

This can become a choice between a rock and a hard place. Consultation threatens design by committee – a notorious supplier of inferior products. Imposition is a shortsighted option at any time, and in this instance risks alienating the people who are supposed to make use of the brochure.

There are some who espouse the direct and dictatorial approach, and drive through a brochure in short time. If a firm has a dogmatic, respected and small management team, to whom responsibility is willingly delegated, this can work. In the vast majority of professional firms, noses would be put out of joint by this *modus operandi*. In view of the complexity of the internal communication task alone, most commentators recommend allowing a minimum of six months to do the job right. Some err on the side of caution and suggest a year and a half!

The compromise solution – brochure production by tact, determination and stealth – also comprises consultation, diplomacy, patience and ruthlessness.

Whatever the case, never start without fixing the brief.

Write a brief

Before writing the first draft, it is essential to take on what may seem an unnecessary and time-consuming task. Write a full brief on what the brochure is supposed to do for the firm and how it should look. Have this brief agreed before work starts on drafting and design. Only then will you realise how well the time spent preparing the brief was invested.

As Don Moorhouse points out, 'there will be disputes. There are inevitably differences of opinion, since everyone has their own strong point of view. Everyone becomes a writer and everyone's a designer when it comes to brochure production'.

Everyone wants it to reflect their own subjective view of the firm – and to some extent their own personality.

Unless there are rules to follow and structures agreed, the brochure will assume an incoherent life of its own. Hence the need for a clear set of objectives and a ruthless hand on the tiller.

For example, it is important to decide whether the format of the brochure should be determined by the wording or the wording by the format. If a visual approach is going to carry the firm's message, then text and the brochure's design and materials will have to be consistent with that approach.

If it is decided that the brochure should be a 16 page A4 creation, it is worth mapping out each page and working out how many words are acceptable for each.

Alternatively, drafting might be the first stage, with appropriate layouts being determined based on the weight of text.

Whichever approach is favoured, there will inevitably be times when there are too many words on a particular page. It is essential to cut the text, rather than amend the format. A brochure has far more to say through clarity of presentation and succinct expression than it does through its written message.

Diplomacy is needed when the sense of this pared down, consistent and disciplined approach is questioned. Some will resent the very existence of the brochure. Others will question the lack of prominence given to their specialisation, or the terminology used to describe their area of practice. Time and patience need to be given to such considerations. Where compromises can be made without affecting the structure of the brochure, make them. If you have to say no to a major change, allow a minor one.

Don't rush. If you are replacing an existing brochure, plan well ahead, so that you have ample time to achieve your goals. If it is a new brochure you are producing, do not commit to a rushed timetable. If the firm has survived this long without a brochure, it can survive until you produce a good one, rather than rattle out a botched job.

It can take many months to gain the acquiescence of everyone in a large partnership. However, once the task has been cracked, you will have a template for all future promotional drafting, design and printing. (This provides a compelling argument for channelling all work through one designer, at least until a corporate identity manual is in existence.)

In addition, and as a considerable bonus, you may find that rather than just reflect the nature of the firm, the brochure goes some way to help shape it. For the first time, everyone can look at a single document and see what the firm thinks it is. For many people, this will be the first time they have seen the firm as anything but a nebulous entity. A good brochure can fix ideas, phrases and identities into the minds of readers, and thus help shape their communication of that firm's nature, structure and strengths.

The limits of consultation

No passion in the world is equal to the passion to alter someone else's draft.

HG Wells

Consultation means allowing everyone the chance to comment on draft text. It does not mean letting them produce their own draft. If the text is to read well, it needs to be the product of a single writer. After that, factual and cosmetic changes should be encouraged, but not stylistic borrowings.

Thus consultation does not mean wholesale acceptance of alterations. This is where ruthlessness comes into play. Any changes which threaten the overall integrity of the brochure must be politely rejected. It may be necessary to explain why. Often, partners will be very happy to have been asked their opinion, and will accept the decision of those in whom responsibility for the brochure has been vested.

If they are not happy, put all your efforts into winning them round. If that does not work, bring in support for your views. If you still face an impasse, do not give in. There has to be a point in brochure production when policy overrules private objections. A failure to achieve consensus must not lead to a failure to produce a clear, homogenous publication.

Drafting

I love being a writer. What I can't stand is the paperwork.

Peter de Vries

What should go into a firm's corporate brochure? Ask 10 people and you will get 10 answers. It is easier to begin with copywriting errors – the absolute no's of brochure writing.

PUBLICATIONS

10 to avoid

- Acres of text. Keep the word count low.
- Puffery. Keep it factual.
- Features of the firm's service. Concentrate on benefits.
- Waffle. Keep it succinct.
- Jargon. The brochure should be comprehensible to the layman.
- Repetition. Avoid paragraphs beginning with the same word and overuse of favourite adjectives.
- Clichés. If you can, eschew words like 'unique' or 'respected' and phrases such as 'vast experience' or 'a wide range'; these are overused, self-congratulatory and look like features rather than benefits.
- Banalities. This brochure is supposed to set you apart. Make sure it avoids 'brochurespeak' and differentiates you.
- Compromise. While there will have to be some leeway given in view of partner preferences, it is vital that the original vision of the copy remains unchanged; the alternative is confused and confusing text.
- Illegalities. Make sure that the text conforms with Law Society guidelines, particularly in respect of client mentions, comparisons and passing off of staff under misleading job descriptions. It costs a lot of money to reprint or correct a brochure.

By keeping copy brief, core messages can be conveyed without the distractions afforded by any of the above errors of judgment.

The tone and content of the copy will depend on the nature of the firm. Since individual style and differentiation must be the objective, there are no diktats to be followed. It is up to each firm to find its own voice.

Try to show how features of the firm work as benefits to clients. Demonstrate through case histories how the expertise and experience of fee earners translates into client advantage. Show how legal advice has prevented problems or won arguments – in other words, give practical examples, not just passive descriptions.

Think about what clients want to read. Sarah Dean tells how Ashurst Morris Crisp's brochure was shaped by 'our designers conducting client research. Under careful supervision, they contacted some of our clients and used the results of these interviews to determine how the brochure should look and read'.

Brochures are usually designed and written by a committee. Invariably, this is a mistake. Since no amount of persuasion will see a firm hand over full authority to write and sign off a draft to a single person within the firm, the services of an objective copywriter are essential.

Leaving it to the firm to generate copy is a guaranteed route to fudge. A flexible yet determined writer is a godsend when producing a brochure. This writer should not only be able to write brochures (a specialist skill) but should be able to think from the client's point of view and thus help determine an appropriate tone and content for the text.

However, a copywriter cannot do the job alone. A recommended route is for such a writer to draft version one, submitting it to the appropriate steering authority. The latter then edits or redrafts after consultation with the partnership.

The copywriter is then brought back into play to bring together a final text. Because this will have moved from his or her initial ideas, no prima donnas can be accommodated. However, part of the writer's role is to manoeuvre the body of work back into a shape which conforms to the original intention.

Fig 15

RECOMMENDED EVOLUTION OF COPY FOR A FIRM'S BROCHURE

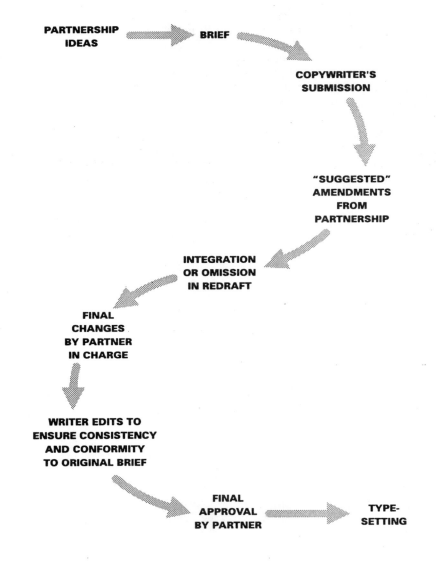

What size should it be?

When producing a corporate brochure, or any publication, you will need to consider its size. This is a decision that can be left to the designer, but it is likely that you will have a view.

Most brochures, newsletters and publicity materials are produced to A4 format, the same size as the average sheet of stationery. A4 is half the size of A3 and twice the size of A5. By extrapolation, the other standard 'A' options can be gauged.

However, few would consider producing an A2 or A6 brochure, so hybrid shapes are worth some thought. Arguments against include the lack of appropriate envelopes for mailing, difficulties of filing or putting in briefcases (large or long shapes), or the tiny type size and impression of insignificance (small versions).

Most firms would be well advised to stick with A4 and A5 formats.

Newsletters

Be careful with these. There are a lot about. Some are good, most are indifferent and some are a waste of time, paper and money.

'The value of a newsletter,' according to Sarah Dean 'is to keep the firm's name to the fore.' Thus it serves to keep the firm in the consciousness of the client or contact. Ashurst Morris Crisp take this to the logical conclusion, with newsletters featuring photographs of fee earners.

However, as Jennie Gubbins of Trowers & Hamlins points out, more important than the 'remember us' role (which is firm-oriented) is 'the need to be informative and client-oriented. If it won't interest the reader, don't run it.'

A newsletter needs to carry news. If this sounds obvious, think of the newsletters you receive. Often, they carry only what the sender thinks of as news. You may find that the publication, either through bad editorial choice or poor targeting, is of no interest; it carries no relevant news.

Before committing yourself to a newsletter, establish who it is intended to reach and research the scope of the mailing. In other words, produce a report on the validity of the exercise in advance. The work entailed in compiling mailing lists will need to be done anyway. It is far better to do this work up front as a means of establishing the feasibility of a newsletter. Such initial research will also enable you to set objectives and establish how to measure success in reaching them.

Anything can go into a newsletter, so long as it passes the test of 'will this be of interest to the reader?'.

As in all law firm initiatives, you will need a staunch advocate who is responsible for the newsletter. Publications which require legal input demand a partner as 'champion'. Ideally, you should have joint editors, one to lead the process and one to back up in particularly busy periods.

These editors are responsible for selecting topical material and coercing contributors. The promotions professional should concentrate on production and editing, and steer clear of drafting copy.

Illustrations are a good idea, but not vital. Newsletters can be ruined by looking less than hardworking. However, tracts of text will need to be leavened by photography, line drawings, cartoons or similar breaks in copy.

Never stray from an agreed format. Overruns of text must be cut. It is folly to reduce the typeface to accommodate verbiage. The impact of a newsletter lies in its consistent values and quality. If different issues look different, you are working against yourself.

While you should never change a typeface to accommodate extra text, there are times when you can alter the consistent nature of a page. This applies to a newsletter, or any other publication.

Lists or quotes can be presented differently (closed up, indented, italicised) to distinguish them or, if necessary, simply to save or use up space. The first letter of a new paragraph can be printed large, to add emphasis and create a sense of importance while visually enlivening the page.

Information vehicles

Consider an alternative to the newsletter if you have briefings to offer clients. Carried in a newsletter, these would lack immediacy and might be tainted by the connotations carried by news sheets of being mere publicity vehicles. Produce a printed document format with serious production values – no extraneous frippery. These can be mailed or displayed as distinct and informative entities, thus achieving the differentiation they require.

Photography and illustrations

Illustrations are important with regard to brightening and punctuating the page, but don't forget that they must communicate as well. Run photographs which tell a story. Avoid those which simply look good. Try not to run pictures of anyone with a phone clamped to her ear or group shots of dozens of people. Try not to cut down images so that you show apparent amputees – though it is acceptable (and wise) to crop any image which shows people's legs dangling under a table.

If you are using photography, ask around. Find work you like and seek out the photographer. Investigate the British Institute of Professional Photography or the Creative Handbook.

When briefing a photographer, bear in mind the following:

Following a change in the law in the late 1980s, the photographer retains copyright on his or her work; if you want to use prints more than once, it would be sensible to come to an initial arrangement.

You cannot get good black and white images from colour photography. Make sure you brief a photographer to shoot in colour and black and white, if you are likely to need both options.

Day rates are unlikely to be less than £500 for an average photographer, and will be nearer £1,000 for an experienced exponent of the art. The rates of 'name' photographers can escalate far higher. Therefore, use your photographer to the full. Plan ahead to cover future requirements, if you can. The extra costs involved in adding subject matter, in terms of film and processing, are small compared to rehiring a photographer.

Professional photographers rarely shoot normal colour film. They use transparencies ('trannies'). This film is more expensive but offers higher definition – 35mm is usually adequate, but if you are contemplating blowing up an image (for use in a poster or on an exhibition stand, for example) tell the photographer. He or she may recommend a larger film format.

Allow time for photography. When you have seen the amount of kit needed for the simplest of professional shoots, you will realise that it can take half a day to photograph a building or capture a few mug shots.

Design and print

Make sure design serves you, not the designer. An over-elaborate publication can repel rather than attract. In most design fields, and particularly in professional services, simplicity, clean lines, legibility and quality must shine through.

The following indicates where design and print might come into play in the production of a typical brochure (if such an entity exists).

Fig 16

PRODUCING A BROCHURE: OUTLINE PROCEDURE

	CLIENT	DESIGNER	PRINTER
START	Agree Project Set Brief Research information Appoint copywriter?		
	Compile copy Brief designer Brief printer Commission designer Commission printer	Research/gather images Produce design roughs Present design ideas	Gather paper samples Show previous work
	Approve paper stock Draft & circulate copy Amend copy Produce final draft	Present detailed design	
	Approve copy Approve typesetting Approve final design	Typeset copy Integrate typesetting into design and present to client Deliver camera-ready artwork	Produce initial proofs
FINISH	Amend/approve proofs Refrain from any further changes Sign-off proofs Distribute		Produce final proofs Print & Deliver

From concept to publication

The above process may map out how you produce a brochure – but then again, it may not. Your input may be sufficiently great to make the designer (and typesetter) redundant, particularly in smaller jobs. Much will depend on what hardware and software you own. If you have nothing but a pen and paper, your designer will earn a lot of money.

Most firms have yet to join the desk top publishing revolution. However, all but the blinkered few now have word-processing. As long as you can save your text onto disk, you will be able to jump several stages of production.

Saving to disk means that you can forward copy which can be professionally typeset directly from the disk. You will next see your text laid out as it should appear on the printed page. The wording should be exactly as you saved it. Thus you are spared the job of proof-reading (though a quick check to eradicate gremlins is wise). This assumes that you have checked copy carefully after initial composition.

Once you have approved the set copy, and any design elements that will be added to the page, your job is largely over. Once the final proof is approved, the page is photographed and the result (camera ready artwork) is forwarded to the printer.

Do it yourself

Such a process evaporates if you have the facilities to desk top publish (DTP).

In 1977, Marshall McLuhan was quoted in the *Washington Post* as saying 'Gutenberg made everybody a reader. Xerox makes everybody a publisher.' Contemporary desk top publishing puts mere photocopying into perspective and indicates that McLuhan was being a little hyperbolic. The revolution is only now taking place – and there are many that will let it pass quietly by.

Those that do take up the opportunities will invariably find that desk top publishing has a useful role to play. Various packages exist, each of which is configured to allow you to design your own pages. You can select required fonts, typeset and lay out the text, scan in photographs or create images and emerge with 'finished' pages.

The only thing you will be unable to do is print these pages yourself. You will, however, be in a position to forward them to a printer as camera ready artwork – ie images of sufficient finished quality for him to print.

Lynn Hill, who now has this facility at Taylor Joynson Garrett, is able to design and take all publications to print stage in-house. This enables her to control the consistent appearance of publications and thus forms part of the corporate identity exercise conducted to eradicate 'a real mish-mash of different styles and formats'.

Whether or not you follow such a desktop procedure will depend on the quality you require from your publication. If you are circulating an internal newsletter, you will probably be able to do without any designer or printer at all, merely photocopying final proofs of pages created within the firm.

However, bear in mind that DTP is uneconomical on long runs.

When producing a client brochure, quality will be lacking if you use desk top publishing. Sometimes, however, it is to your advantage to use a less 'glossy' process. Briefing sheets, for example, may look better without the high production values of external printing.

When choosing a DTP package, look out for quality and speed of output, the quality of half tones (shaded images), the capacity to produce colour, how easy it is to make up pages, the options to expand performance and the ease with which images can be scanned onto a page. Scanners are cheap and effective tools, which work by copying and then transferring images from an external source to your page. An investment in scanning can transform a workhorse into a thoroughbred.

Ensure that you have a laser printer of at least 600 DPI (dots per inch) quality and that it can print out A3 sheets. This will enable you to produce A4 folded booklets or newsletters.

Typesetters

The chapter on advertising explains the role played by typesetters. If you are producing a brochure without your own DTP typesetting input, you will need specialist setters. Traditionally, a service offered by printers, (type)setting can also be bought as a separate service, or, through the wonders of the Apple Mac and various software packages, direct from your designer.

It is advisable to make this process as invisible as possible. Don't get involved directly. This is not to say that the setting is irrelevant. A skilled typesetter can do a far more professional job using much more sophisticated technology than you can. However, it is largely a mechanical process which should be channelled through your designer.

The simplest means of operating is to find a team who work together, either as a single entity or through loose affiliation. If the latter case applies, find a designer who can project-manage, so that he or she can take and convert your brief into a finished document. You really do not want to spend your time as a relay service between the typesetter, designer and printer. Without abrogating control or losing touch with what is happening, you can save time, confusion and effort through shortening the lines of communication.

Choosing your typeface

There are thousands of typefaces to choose from. Resist them. Select and use only two or three typefaces and err on the side of simplicity at all times. Using too many will make you look like a child with a Letraset, or the writer of a ransom note.

Typefaces are also known as fonts. Different fonts can communicate distinct tones and moods, but one can become over mystical about these hidden messages. If it feels right, it probably is.

If you do mix them make sure that you mix them unsubtly. Using two similar styles will look sloppy – as if you had not noticed the difference. Try putting a serif with a sans serif (serifs are the fiddly pointed bits at the extremes of letters; sans serif typefaces are much cleaner and simpler).

Jargon

Designers and typesetters may bamboozle you with jargon. Don't accept this. Demand that they speak in standard English, not their arcane branch of the language. However, if they persist, the following may come in useful.

If someone refers to the 'weight' of text, this means the thickness of the letters, which range from ultra light to extra bold. 'Form' means the style of lettering (ie bold, or italic).

A point is one seventy-second of an inch. If you hear the phrase 'point size' this simply means the size of the text. The higher the number, the larger the size. Anything lower than 14 point is usually body copy (ie standard text) while anything larger is probably a headline or similar.

Line spaces are defined through point size ie 10/11 simply means that the line of text takes up a defined amount of room (10 point), with the spacing between it and the next line taking up exactly the same amount of room plus a single extra point of additional spacing, known as 'leading' (pronounced 'ledding').

Spacing between the letters in a word may be described as 'condensed', 'expanded' or 'customised'. Each means exactly what it appears to mean!

Text may be 'justified' to both the left and right margins, so that each line of text begins and ends at the same place, resulting in flush margins. Alternatively, text may be unjustified, which means that either the left or right side is 'ragged'. In practice this usually means that it is the right hand margin which is left ragged. Other options are to centre each line, or to adopt a creative 'asymmetrical' layout.

The length of each line is known as its 'measure', with the maximum measure being the length of the longest permissible line on the page.

Colour

As the diagram at the beginning of this chapter shows, colour can have a dramatic effect on the cost of a publication. Most people assume that a straight choice exists between black and white or full colour (rather like standard photography). In fact, powerful effects and worthwhile cost savings can be made through creative use of print processes.

If your budget stretches to one colour only, the normal approach is to print this single colour solidly (100%) onto the paper stock. However, variety or effect can be achieved through printing a tint (from 5% (light) through to 95% (dark)) of this single colour. Alternatively, you can 'surprint' – printing over a tinted background. A fourth option is to 'reverse' the text out of a solid colour (or lightly tinted) background.

Adding a second colour allows additional creative options, such as adding a percentage tint of the second colour to provide a lift and added interest in a black and white photograph.

However, if you want to reproduce colour photography accurately, you will need to use four colour process printing. Confusingly, this is not the same as four colour printing.

The latter restricts you to four colours only, in the same way that three colour uses (you guessed it) only three colours. Four colour process printing uses 'separations' of four special colours (black, yellow, cyan (blue) and magenta (red)) to reproduce the full spectrum of colours.

When printing, each colour you use has to be run through the print process separately on its own plate. That is why the origination process can become so expensive. However, plates can be reused (provided you do not change elements) so reprinting is never as expensive as starting from scratch.

Proofs and the printing process

As the client, you want to see what you are going to get from the job, before you get it. This is achieved through proofs. You will see these in different forms at different stages.

The printer will work from 'mechanicals' – designers' proofs. Different printers will then offer you an array of delicacies: laser proofs, galleys, ozalids, chromalins and so forth.

In the continuing battle to get specialists to speak simply and comprehensibly, tell them you are not interested in these meaningless terms. Impress on them only your need to check everything at each stage – then ask them to tell you what and when those stages are. Ensure that they help you to your objective by adding their recommendations. Explain to them that you want to know what you can expect to see when and what extra costs, if any, are incurred through your doing so.

Usually, you will see black and white proofs to check that you are happy with the layout and that all the indefinables of the pages 'look right'. Here you can make changes with relative impunity. You will have to pay for all changes occasioned by you, but the figures should not be unreasonable. Ensure that you do not get charged for printer or designer errors.

By the time you start seeing proofs in colour, you should be warned that any changes you make will require you to pay through the nose. Unless the colour reproduction is wrong, alter nothing and treat this as it is intended: a chance to reassure yourself that the pages look as they should.

This does not mean you should accept any faults from the design process, or approve copy if you still have reservations. As Don Moorhouse, managing partner of Trowers & Hamlins, stresses, 'it is vital that the final stage of proofing gives you an exact example of what you will see on the printed page – a WYSIWYG proof showing 'what you see is what you get'. Only then should you feel confident enough to give instructions to print.'

Going to print

When it comes to the printing process, you can either take an interest and become an expert, or do what most sensible clients do and relax. Printing is a complex and messy job (though less so than it once was). Restrict yourself to complaining when the results are inferior, or buying the printer a drink if all works to plan.

If you must know more about what is taking place, you will find that in most cases your documents are being produced through an offset lithographic process. In the case of single colour printing, your artwork is turned into a line negative and half tones are stripped in. The negative is transferred onto flexible metal plates (the litho plates) which are coated in light-sensitive chemicals.

Developed like photographs, these plates are then coated with chemicals which either attract or repel water or ink. This ensures that the right parts take up the image to be created. This image is 'offset' onto rubber blankets, being reversed in the process, and then re-reversed as the blanket prints the image onto paper.

In the case of colour, and simplifying hugely, the same process takes place for each colour used, with an image being built up through superimposition.

Readers are warned that it is inadvisable to try this at home.

Other printing options

If you are producing exhibition panels, pencils, umbrellas or printing on glass or a non-flat surface, you may find yourself using screen printing. This is essentially a stencilling process. A raised effect can be achieved through embossing (squashing paper between dyes) or thermography (using powder which adheres to ink).

Since it is unlikely that you will be printing more than one million copies of any document, we will leave the mysteries of gravure printing unexplored.

100

Choosing your paper stock

Most publications use coated stock – paper coated in a fine clay compound to seal the surface. This looks crisp, enhances contrast and provides sharp line definition. A matt finish is good for text, in that there is no reflected glare from the page, while gloss can enhance the colours in a photograph. Gloss is also often cheaper.

The thickness of your stock is measured in gsm, or grammes per square metre. For a quality brochure cover, you will want around 220 gsm or more – up to 300 gsm for a stiffish folder. Your professional stationery is probably around 90 or 100 gsm; aim for at least this thickness in selecting paper for use within a brochure, and preferably something closer to 135-160gsm.

If you are using a gloss cover, make sure that it is laminated against finger marks.

Often, highly finished brochures with glossy covers arrive dog-eared on a recipient's desk. While considering the format of your brochure or publication, talk to the designer and printer about the need, if any, for packaging. They may have ideas which can protect items from damage.

Binding

Nine times out of ten you will be best off using saddle stitching. This puts staples through the central crease of the open document to hold anything up to around 64 pages together.

In a bulkier document, perfect binding is a popular option. One eighth of an inch is sheared off the margins, creating a roughened effect. Glue is added and the document is heat bound into a preprinted cover. Optionally, a reinforcing cloth spine contains the pages before binding into the cover.

The advantage of this heat sealed option is that it is largely invisible and usually effective. Contrary factors include the fact that document size needs to be known in order to determine spine width and allow the preprinting of covers.

Additionally, the publication's pages will not lie flat and any text inadvertently printed too close to the inside margin may be obscured. Poor workmanship will result in single pages coming free, though if this happens the printer/binder has a case to answer.

Case binding is the Rolls Royce option. Paper is folded into sets which are then sewn into the spine of a hard cover. The first and last sheets are then glued to endpapers. Paper is then trimmed to shape and the spine reinforced. This allows spines to be rounded or flat, covers to be paper or board, and the addition of leather, cloth or paper covers.

Stabwiring is a crude method of holding a document together. A strip of plastic is attached to toggles on the opposite side of the manuscript by means of prongs 'shot' through the document. Similarly, side-stitching wires together staples shot through the document, about 5mm from the edge. In both cases, a cover is overglued to hide the evidence.

Finally, there is a range of cheap mechanical binding options, ranging from plastic combs, metal spirals, double loops and ring binders. Most of these options are used in-house, to prepare handouts for seminars and client documentation. These workmanlike options are excellent for the everyday, but should be avoided when presentation standards are deemed important.

The print run

A perennial problem when producing publications lies in print runs. How many copies of any publication are going to be required?

Obviously this depends on the use to which they are put, the opportunities to distribute them, and the enthusiasm with which members of the firm promote them. Each firm will find correct print run numbers after a few years. But how should they set an initial figure?

The following is open to charges of bovine over-simplification, but may provide a starting point.

The chances are that few partners will use more than 100 brochures a year. A firm of 10 might only require a print run of 1,000, while a hundred-strong partnership would find perhaps 8,000 brochures sufficient for one year's use. Obviously, figures will rise if high profile events or mailings are contemplated.

Why one year? Should you not produce enough brochures to last two years, or revise copy every six months to reflect topical issues?

Do you produce a format that allows the use of inserts, so that unchanging core copy can be topped and tailed on a regular basis? Do you include names or photographs of partners, risking forced reprints if partners then leave the firm?

102

MARKETING COMMUNICATIONS FOR SOLICITORS _____

There are no stock answers to these questions. However, they need to be raised so that a brochure is produced within a planned approach. This means that revisions and reprints follow a pattern, rather than require new thinking at each turn.

A huge amount of money is thrown away on brochure production through ordering too many or too few copies. The safest approach is to err on the side of too many, having established a format that guarantees longevity. That means keeping partner names out of the body copy. It means leaving out any reference that will date the copy. It means providing a flap or device to contain inserts, if such are needed to provide a topical focus to the brochure in subsequent years.

Don't cut print runs in the hope of saving equivalent sums. A 50% cut in the run will probably save between 10 and 30%, the lower figure being more likely. This is because it is the initiation process which eats up most of your print budget, through plate making, proofing and associated esoteric activities. Once a job is on the presses, particularly in the case of a simple document, it may actually make little or no difference to the cost whether you print 5,000 or 10,000.

Run ons

If you ask for quotes for a print job, you may be given a figure for the 'run-ons'. If you are quoted £2,000 for 10,000 leaflets, with a run on of £86 per 1,000, this means that every additional 1,000 you want to add to the original 10,000 will cost you £86.

Conversely, if you decide to order less copies, subtract £86 for each 1,000 by which you reduce the original 10,000 on which the quote was based. Thus you would expect to pay £1,914 for 9,000 copies.

These figures endorse the point made above, about how much of print costs relate to setting up a job, and how little can be saved even by dramatically reducing print runs. If, using the above example, you choose to reduce the run by 4,000 and thus print only 6,000 copies, you would reduce the quote by £344 (4 x £86) to £1,656.

This would result in a per-leaflet cost of 28p, whereas the per-leaflet cost on a full run of 10,000 would be 20p. In effect, you have 'saved' just over £300, 'lost' 4,000 leaflets and increased the per item cost by almost 50%.

103

Summary

- In a promotional brochure, form is more important than content. Only when conveying factual and immediately relevant information does the balance reverse.
- Never produce a publication unless you are clear on how it is to be used and distributed.
- Publications should always follow a corporate identity, or failing this, a series of consistent guidelines to ensure uniformity.
- Costing publications without firm rules on the variables is largely impossible. Either set a limit and find out what your money can buy, or arrange a costing exercise only when all variables have been fixed.
- Consult the partnership but make it clear that you retain full editorial control and the power of veto.
- Allow a great deal of time to the production process. A brochure produced in a hurry rarely works.
- Drafting should be done by one person. Editing should be handled by one person. Only the in-between process should admit of committee/partnership amendments.
- Copy should be brief, factual and of more interest to the reader than the writer. It should be crisp and cliché-free. If a 100 word brochure conveys core strengths, why write 2,000 words?
- Determine a format (size and materials).
- Write a brief, to guide progress and justify decisions made.
- Write a timetable.
- Don't run newsletters unless they contain information useful to a known mailing list. Research and clean up your list if you are in doubt.
- Make sure that newsletters have staunch advocates within departments.
- Keep the appearance consistent. Cut text rather than change typesize.
- Use illustrations to tell a story or break up text – but not just because they look good.
- Cover several jobs at once if you are hiring a photographer. Day or half-day rates are high. Allow time for photography – it is a slow process.
- If you need colour and black and white images, tell the photographer in advance. If you have a requirement and are not sure how to brief the photographer, give details and ask for recommendations

MARKETING COMMUNICATIONS FOR SOLICITORS

and costs.
- Employ only designers who understand the importance of under-statement and keeping things clean and simple.
- Relay copy to a typesetter/designer on disk, when possible.
- Consider investing in a desktop publishing (DTP) package. This can save time and money in the long run. You will be able to send camera ready artwork direct to printers, saving design and setting costs.
- DTP is, however, uneconomical on long runs. Design standards will fall short of those achieved by the professionals. DTP is not a replacement for external help.
- Use a scanner to add photography, cartoons and diagrams to newsletters produced on DTP.
- Obtain a good laser printer; a poor one will make the advantages of DTP redundant.
- Arrange external typesetting via your designer, if possible.
- Choose your typefaces from the corporate identity manual, or, if this does not exist, based on simplicity. Avoid the 'letraset' approach.
- Don't allow suppliers to bamboozle you with jargon. Do not proceed until matters have been explained to you in plain English and you have understood time, quality and cost implications.
- Note the effect colour has on print costs. Explore half tones as an alternative to additional colour usage.
- Ask to see proofs. Make sure that the final proofs show exactly what will be seen on the pages printed.
- Try not to interfere in the printing process, but reject any work that does not conform to the final proofs.
- Ask to see stock samples before you approve cover and content paper.
- Consider how publications will be used before deciding on paper quality and protective coverings.
- Ensure that you are clear as to which binding method will be used on the brochure before approving print details.
- Anticipate usage to determine print run. Err on the side of timeless text and long runs.
- Do not cut print runs to save money. It is usually a false economy.

Hints and tips

- Try to put several jobs through together. This saves money.

- Before establishing a format or brief, ask to see print samples. This can help you determine what you do and do not want from your commission.
- Keep your partners and staff in all offices informed about what is available and which documents have been updated. Only then will they be widely used. Ensure old copies are thrown away.
- Display all publications in reception.
- Send informative publications to the media, or adapt them into articles.
- Centralise all print production. If other offices follow their noses, they are unlikely to follow all guidelines.
- Consider producing clip files or folders for newsletters, for client use.
- Review the effectiveness of newsletters. Attach a questionnaire with reply-paid mechanism, to elicit constructive criticism and views on what does and does not get read.
- Make sure that more than one name is given as a point of contact on a publication. A single name implies less resources; additionally, that person may be unavailable when an enquiry is made.

6 Speaking in public

I am the most spontaneous speaker in the world because every word, every gesture and every retort has been carefully rehearsed.

George Bernard Shaw

If someone compiled a list of areas where the professions could do themselves greater justice, giving presentations might well top the list. I would suggest that, whilst most people present poorly, professionals can be worse than poor.

This is not necessarily the professional's fault. Lawyers, accountants et al are trained to master a subject, marshal information into facts, and cover every inch of ground.

In building their practice, it is a straightforward matter to provide what is required. The process is a linear one, from the brief to completion of a task, by way of documents and detail.

So it is hardly surprising that, when given the task of speaking formally, the professions adopt their trusted techniques.

They dump information, in a dull, factual deluge (I generalise). They give monotonous read-throughs of pre-chewed text. They stare glassily at notes, which chart a course from lifeless introduction to deflated finale.

All but the best fail to present: they read.

It does not have to be so. A good presentation is not impossible to achieve. It does require a mind open enough to accept that techniques have to be learned. As Cristina Stuart, managing director of presentation training specialists SpeakEasy, points out, 'contrary to some opinion, good speakers are mad, not born. This means that lawyers, who are usually already masters of the language, need to have the humility to accept that there are lessons that need learning and new rules to be followed'.

These rules apply to formal and substantial presentations (conferences, seminars) and to formal, smaller gatherings (beauty parades, workshops). However, most of the points covered remain valid for any form of interaction. Most of us need to learn anew, or for the first time, how to communicate from the recipient's point of view.

So what are the rules?

Tailor to time

Make sure you approach the presentation based on the time you have available to talk and the tone you are required to adopt. Don't give a short summary to a formal gathering, and never prepare a half hour presentation for a 20 minute slot.

Think from the audience's point of view – not your own

At the risk of belabouring the point until it can barely stand, as in all forms of successful communication, it is more important to consider what your audience wants to hear than what you want to say.

People want to know how things affect them, not merely that they have happened. Indicate the benefits or threats, not the features of a recent development.

Use the active rather than the passive, the example, not the flat description.

If your audience wants to hear all you know on a subject, resist the temptation to accommodate them. They will be overwhelmed by facts.

That's what your notes are for.

Sell yourself – not your subject

The simple truth is that you are never, ever, on a podium, behind a lectern or on your feet simply to convey information. That is secondary. Every time you are called on to address an audience, you are selling yourself.

In the world of the professional, this sounds ludicrous. Partners are not entertainers. Audiences want to gain information, not listen to someone on an ego trip.

The flaw here is that, however much an audience wants to ignore the speaker and absorb the speech, such a course is impossible to take. We are constitutionally unable to take in most of what we hear.

If you remember one thing from this chapter, let it be the preceding sentence.

Many people in the legal world focus only on the need to convey facts. They fail to think about how an audience assimilates a message. Audiences do not absorb information like sponges. The majority of speakers assume they do.

Try to remember a talk given two months ago and you'll recall a tiny percentage. Even on leaving a lecture hall, most people can recall only a fraction of what was said.

Yet all will recall their impressions of the speaker.

Not just that day. Years later.

A now-famous US study into how audiences respond to presentations came to the conclusion that more than half (58%) of the audience's reaction derived from perceptions of the speaker's body language. A further 35% arose from reactions to voice (tone, pace, modulations and inflections, warmth, etc). That left only 7% arising from the content of the speech.

AUDIENCE PERCEPTION: THE RELATIVE UNIMPORTANCE OF CONTENT WHEN CREATING A POSITIVE IMPRESSION

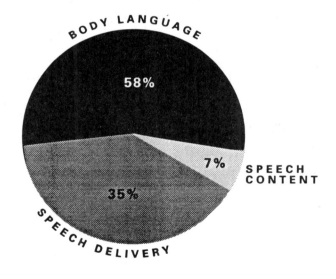

Fig 17

Think about this. It probably runs counter to everything you have ever believed. The impact of your presentation is less than one tenth dependant on what you have to say.

If you choose to disbelieve this finding (the author has no evidence to show that the findings are irrefutable), you are likely to fall into the safe but shallow haven where addresses are content-dominated. These never do what they are designed to do. If you focus on what to say to the exclusion of how to win over your audience, you may win plaudits – you may even gain some work – but you will miss bigger prizes and will not do yourself or your firm justice.

This point holds true in relation to even the most fact-hungry delegates at a conference. Just as they may delude themselves that facts are all they want, so most speakers connive by presenting unleavened information which is promptly forgotten.

Commenting on such an approach, Jenkin Lloyd Jones famously damned the perpetrator. 'A speech,' he points out, 'is a solemn responsibility. The man who makes a bad 30-minute speech to 200 people only wastes half an hour of his own time. But he wastes 100 hours of the audience's time – more than four days —which should be a hanging offence.'

You don't have to get in the way of your material – merely bring it to life.

Keep it simple

It is infinitely preferable to keep things simple. State your agenda before you start. Put across a few points only, summarising, exemplifying and repeating. The latter is important. The old adage enjoins one to 'say what you are going to say, say it, then say it again.' This should be up in lights in every conference or seminar venue in the land.

Only through repetition will your message be conveyed and remembered.

Tell or sell?

Decide if you are speaking to inform or persuade. If it is the former, build your presentation around that single most important piece of information you wish to impart. If you are trying to persuade your audience, ensure you specify what action you want them to take.

Getting started

Don't ever accept an invitation to talk on a subject unless you are confident you know enough about it. Just as a good presentation can enhance reputation, a poor one can waste it – along with time and effort.

110

If invited to speak, ensure that all parties are clear on the subject matter to be covered. Then get out that blank sheet of paper.

Rather than write out your speech, jot down at random key words or phrases. Put your central theme in the middle of the page, surrounding it by the elements you would like to cover. Use arrows to link together the disparate phrases and ideas.

Once this has been done, confirm that the central theme is the one you wish to build the talk around. Remember that your audience will only remember the main point of your talk, and perhaps two or three subsidiary points, so it is important to build everything in your presentation around these structures.

Weed out the clever bits you want to include, but which don't fit this pared down approach.

Now you can look to order the talk into a sequence.

Try to shape it into an introduction, the presentation itself divided into three equal sections, and the conclusion. By all means ditch this structure as you go, but put your material into such compartments at the planning stage. You now have the core material. What is essential, now, is the addition of vitality.

Paint pictures; inject life

There is no audience so august that it will not respond to the injection of life into your talk. Most of this will come from your delivery and demeanour, on which there will be more shortly. However, there is always room for bolstering your core material with a little vibrancy. Try adding the following:

Adjectives and adverbs. Idiom and hyperbole. Metaphors and similes. Examples and anecdotes. Enthusiasm.

You can be speaking fascinating truths about statutory obligations, financial instruments or conveyancing fraud, but your words will only be remembered and believed if you present with enthusiasm.

Read the next paragraph, aloud.

'The future for firms in this market will be difficult. Lawyers will discover that new prospects become hard to find. Most of us will need to use our marketing resources to the full, research each opportunity as never before, prior to taking those opportunities that do arise. There will be opportunities, but only the best prepared firms will be in a position to gain additional work.'

Now try this version:

SPEAKING IN PUBLIC

'Those lawyers who once trod water are now drowning. If you don't move, you sink. Those who fail to recognise that aggression is needed in a competitive market will go under. Yet dry land is still in reach. Those that compete on price, on quality, through new products – and above all on service – will never find themselves short of clients.'

The latter may not be perfect. The analogy may look forced in print. But I can assure any doubting reader that read out it would knock spots off its pale twin. It is almost impossible to imbue the first version with emphasis, with passion.

'But we're not in the business of conveying passion.'

Nonsense. The purpose of every presentation is to motivate. The honest end result of every presentation is a sale: more work for the firm. If it is not, then something is wrong with the planning process.

The best means of gaining work is not through a luke-warm client. It is through an enthusiastic client. One who has been won over by an authoritative, informative presentation – for there must be information, of course – but more importantly, one who has been motivated.

You cannot motivate through facts alone. It is the duty of the speaker to be interesting, to present opportunities to the audience, to explain implications, to demonstrate enthusiasm, to paint such a picture of events that all present want to investigate further, in the presence of such an involved and prescient authority.

Break down the divide

The transformation is often astonishing. You are chatting to a colleague, whose wit is not in doubt, whose company charming, whose knowledge is profound. Suddenly she is called upon to speak. What happens?

She changes into a paragon of formality. Dryness descends upon her like a shroud. Her natural modulation of her conversation is lost in the characterless tones of lecture.

The reasons are partly to do with convention and partly derived from the fear we all feel when called upon to speak. Convention dictates a mode and tone of address, 'appropriate' to formal presentations. The fact that it is usually totally inappropriate to communication is ironic.

There is a feeling that legal matters require a sober and formal approach. Quite right. But communicating on the subject does not. When addressing a large group, even if they are your peers or superiors, there is absolutely no reason why the seriousness of a subject cannot be conveyed through being entertaining as well as instructive. This does not mean becoming a comedian. Telling a joke is one of the riskiest things you can do in a presentation.

Additionally, fear drives us in on ourselves. Where we should be breaking down barriers between speakers and audiences, we erect as many as we can through self preservation.

Hence most speakers find eye contact difficult. Yet this is essential. Eye contact is a form of rapport, an acknowledgement of importance. Without it, no speaker is communicating properly.

Ironically, poor speakers try to avoid the natural rhythms of speech, for fear that this will create contact. What they want is to get the ordeal over with as fast as possible. What they need, by contrast, is to slow down and establish the contact that they fear.

Format, not content

The answer to this dilemma is to concentrate less on content and more on format – the style, tone, delivery and 'feel' of a talk. The best speakers associate their audience with a presentation. They use enveloping phrases, like 'as we might suspect' or 'how does this affect all of us here?'. They might refer to members of the audience, in passing. They draw up hypothetical scenarios to exemplify a point, in which sections of the audience represent alternative views. The audience needs not say a word, but they are imaginatively involved.

The speaker's eye contact holds their attention, in much the same way that a teacher's holds that of schoolchildren.

This analogy may seem trite, but it is accurate. Just as the pupil's wavering attention is focused by a gimlet eye, so the conference delegate's attention can be maintained by eye contact.

It is not that the delegate fears being caught out in the way a pupil might (though there may be a subconscious echo of this). More importantly, no delegate has a constant attention span. They need to be actively engaged, through eye contact, rather than left alone. It is up to the speaker to realise this, and address the problem.

Audience attention spans

Most people can only concentrate intensely for about seven minutes. Then the mind takes a breather. It wanders off for a moment, before returning refreshed for another short burst of close attention.

SPEAKING IN PUBLIC

The speaker who is aware of this takes action. He or she places attention grabbers throughout a talk, to ensure that delegates' 'rest periods' do not extend for too long (at worst, throughout a talk).

Eye contact is one method. Hypothetical questions asked of the audience works to the same effect. The extended pause, followed by a challenging statement is another option. Each serves to engage or re-engage attention.

Just as attention levels rise and dip throughout a talk, there is a pattern to a series of talks, perhaps at a conference. As a new speaker shapes to address the gathering, there is a surge of attention. This is a fabulous opportunity. Start badly and you are lost. Begin powerfully – with a challenging statement, a clear exposition of your central theme, a wry comment, or similar – and you have made an impression that will last.

Equally, attention levels rise dramatically at the end of a talk. How do people know you are finishing? Because it says so in the programme? Possibly. This is one major reason not to overrun. It taxes the patience of people waiting for you to finish. No, the way an audience should be alerted to your intention of winding up is for you to tell them.

By explicitly stating that you are moving to your summary or conclusion, you can ride out the remainder of your talk on a wave of interest. Here, the audience expects, is the core of the talk packaged in summary form. Don't disappoint them. Ensure that you sum up the key theme and message of the talk. The last words you say should be designed to be taken from the building and pondered by delegates.

This 'signposting' is not just a function of the closing moments of a talk. Explaining what you have just said, where it takes you, and what needs to be addressed next, is a marvellous technique. It reclaims lost listeners. All too often, the speaker, embroiled in his mastery of the subject, loses passengers early on and careers through the rest of his journey without presenting any opportunity for co-travellers to climb aboard. Thus these mini-summaries serve to ram home key messages, while providing a chance for those who have lost the thread to pick up the pace once again.

Preparation and practice

It is a fine idea to write out and learn a powerful opening paragraph. This will ensure impact as you try to make an initial impression. It will also give you time to settle into your talk.

114

By all means write out the rest of the speech. On no account, however, should you use this version. Practice with it until you are confident that you could finish each paragraph, if given the right cue. Then note these cue words or phrases (never more) on a series of cards.

These words then serve as prompts, bringing back memories of the paragraphs semi-learned in practice. They allow you to unleash the full force of your personality, by freeing you from slavish adherence to a set text.

The usual worry here is that the speaker will lose his way. The response is to stress the importance of practice. Rehearse enough, and you cannot fail. No one invited onto a platform dries up in everyday debate or conversation: therefore, by using the right techniques, there is no reason why you should not be able to control nerves and give an apparently impromptu talk.

The alternative, of taking screeds of A4 notes into a presentation, has several disadvantages.

Chief among these is the obvious one: that when reading from such notes, you cannot be interacting with your listeners. Few make the correlation with everyday speech, where (in the Western world) we would all feel offended if someone failed to meet our eye in conversation. The way most presentations are conducted implies that looking at the listener is not important in a formal situation.

Reading from a script, unless you are a professional actor or broadcaster, sounds dead. No matter how many times you raise your eyes, such a presentation will always be stilted, in comparison to a free-flowing talk based on reading key words from cue cards.

If the notes are left on a lectern, they prevent movement around the presentation area. Using small cards allows the speaker to move about, using the cards as prompts. Large sheets of paper preclude this: they rustle, fold, stand out and – if the speaker's hands shake – they quiver. Slight hand shakiness can be invisible; magnified down the length of a sheet of paper, it can look positively palsied.

Giving the speech

Because people suffer from nerves, so do most presentations. Speaking in public ranks high in most people's pantheon of business horrors. The result is the aforementioned stilted, formal and conservative style.

You will never conquer nerves, but you can get them to serve you. A rush of adrenaline can open up channels of enthusiasm, rather than batten down the hatches.

115

It is important to relax into the talk. Breathing exercises play their part and some favour anything from the Alexander technique to reciting mantras. Less exotic is convincing yourself that you cannot fail.

Firstly, you know more about your subject than anyone in the audience. If you do not, you certainly know enough to steer the session. You are giving a monologue, in which only you know the running order. No one has the right to interrupt (unless you choose to allow this). You are in control.

The audience is a friend, not an enemy. People are there to learn from you. They do not want you to fail: that would waste their time (and perhaps money).

If the audience is senior to you, or composed of authority figures, bring it down to scale. Imagine the most awesome individuals as infants, or wearing ridiculous underwear. Anything to restore a sense of reality, where you are in control.

Usually, people speed up their delivery when nervous. If this is true for you, make a conscious effort to speak slowly. Your pace may seem artificially slow to you, but it will not to the audience. Write the word 'slow' on your cue cards and breathe deeply before you are due to speak.

The pause should be used by all speakers. It is an immensely effective way of refocusing attention. It gives you the chance to marshal your thoughts for the next section of your talk. And it provides an opportunity to start the next sentence with punch. Having ended the pre-pause sentence by lowering your voice, you can start the next on a slightly higher register.

Try this. Out loud. You should find that it serves to interrupt what might otherwise become a monotonous delivery.

Visual aids

Visual aids should be just that – visual representations of things that cannot easily be explained. Too much text on an overhead projector can distract rather than help. A page full of numbers serves no purpose other than to bemuse. By all means put key figures onto a screen or flip-chart, but make sure that they are straightforward and simple. Never reproduce printed matter or computer print-outs as visual aids.

Use slides and all visual aids sparingly. Just as it is a cardinal sin to produce slides with tranches of text on them, it is also a prime offence to use a size of text that cannot be seen by the shortsighted or those at the back of the auditorium.

116

Visual aids should be used to show or reinforce the structure of a talk. If it is essential that complex information be imparted visually, work to keep such information as simple to follow as possible. Err on the side of simplification rather than comprehensive detail.

Slides should never be used to repeat what you have said. Show a slide or overhead projection with this intention in mind, and your audience will direct all their attention to the visual and none to your audio. Why bother speaking when it is on the screen?

However, they serve a useful purpose in backing up the signposting of your talk. Use them to reflect where you are in the structure of your presentation. In this guise they become the backbone or the talk and help to break material up into digestible and differentiated segments.

If you must produce bullet points which mirror your monologue, make sure that they do not do so exactly. If your slide says 'Implications for the plaintiff' ensure that you say something along the lines of 'so, what should the plaintiff anticipate happening next?'

Financial information, corporate structures, market share, projected growth or decline, relationships – these are the rightful subjects for visual aids.

Your visual display is more interesting than you are. Show your slide, let the audience take it in, then either ignore it, or better still, take it off screen. Turning to talk to the slide is fatal. Presented with your back, the audience will accept the invitation to fall into a quiet slumber.

Many presentations have been ruined by mix ups over visuals. Practice using them. Check the running order. Number code the slide or acetate. Make sure you know how to adjust the focus, lay out an overhead, reverse through your slides. There is no substitute for a run through, a full dress rehearsal.

Your demeanour and appearance

How dare this character tell me how to appear?!

To some extent, such indignation is fair enough. Professionals dress well. I would not expect anyone to arrive at a speaking engagement with tousled hair, tie askew, dress cut too low or with filthy glasses.

Yet it happens.

If you look bad, you are assumed to be less competent. Obvious, but often forgotten. Anyone responsible for selecting speakers should make a point of averting disaster on the day by asking about intentions with regard to personal appearance. Speakers should dress as if for a meeting with a senior client.

Jackets should be worn and buttoned. Shoe polish should have come into recent contact with shoes. Loose change or keys should be left with any bulky items in an ante-room or briefcase – never in pockets.

Equally important is your demeanour. Here we go back to the problem engendered by speaking opportunities. We see them as formal and become stuffy. We decide that a smile would trivialise the important subject matter we are trying to convey.

Now if you were to break into an inane grin, or throw in an off-colour joke, there would be a problem. Mid-way between inappropriate levity and dreary solemnity lies your personality. Let it loose.

Use your everyday good humour. Lighten your colloquialisms with a smile. The impression of authority, relaxed good humour and enthusiasm is a potent combination.

A relaxed mien can be taken too far, however. Hands in pockets may (arguably) be all right for the chairman, but the attitude struck usually looks cocky. What is worse, it traps one of your best means of physical communication, second only to eye contact in importance. Your arms.

Body language

Your body is more honest than your tongue. In communication, we all recognise that, even if we do not acknowledge it consciously. Thus an audience is often more interested in what your body is saying, than what your mouth utters.

Therefore, it is important to ensure that your body language mirrors and supports your message. If you are referring to something important, grand or extensive, use your arms and hands in a gesture that reflects size. If you are alluding to a tiny problem, depict something small between your index fingers.

If something upsets you, show it. Remember Kruschev banging his shoe at the UN? Bang your proverbial shoe. Equally, if you are excited about something, don't stand rigid behind a lectern – show that your are pleased about this development.

How often have you heard some talk of 'an exciting opportunity' in a voice from the grave, emanating from a rigid body? The message? Unequivocal: 'I don't believe this myself'.

If you are seen fiddling with your mouth and not using your hands to make natural gestures, there is a fair chance the audience will think you are lying. Why? Because studies have shown that this is how we react when we lie. So make sure that you use proper presentation techniques to counter any subconscious impressions an audience may be receiving.

Unchain yourself from the false protection of your lectern or desk. Arrange to be fitted with a radio microphone. Walk around, make gestures.

The English have nothing to fear. As an undemonstrative race, we will feel we are overplaying our hand when we will hardly have moved. If you are closer to a Mediterranean line of descent and temperament, then you may have to restrain the gestures.

Some people, conscious that they should be using their hands, twitch from the wrist. The effect is offputting, making the twitcher look like an absurdly small-winged bird trying to fly. Use whole arm gestures, allowing your natural demonstrativeness to come to the fore.

Ending well

End on a summary of your key points. As SpeakEasy's Cristina Stuart explains, 'Attention levels rise at the end of a talk, so make it clear that you are finishing, by stating 'in conclusion', 'in summary' or similar. This will heighten the attention of your audience, giving you the opportunity to repeat your main message and fix it in their minds.'

Questions

Why are we afraid of presentations? Because we think we are going to look stupid. How will that happen?

Any number of ways, we believe, but the worst is facing aggressive questioning from someone who has spotted flaws in your argument.

Partial reassurance derives from the infrequency that this happens. Usually, you will know the answers; usually, questions are constructive.

However, there are times when the speaker is put on the spot. Dealing with such situations can make the difference between leaving the audience with a positive or a negative impression.

The golden rule is never to commit professional suicide by arguing with the questioner in front of the rest of the audience. Also, avoid trying

SPEAKING IN PUBLIC

to answer a question when you do not know the answer. Blustering, embarrassment and a loss of credibility will be the usual result.

It is also worth noting that trying to cut the questioner down to size rarely works. An obviously snide or aggressive question will put the audience on your side; you will score highly if you can extricate yourself without trampling on the inquisitor. Fighting back is likely to transfer sympathies to your victim.

So do you avoid the question? No again. This merely frustrates all present. The answer is to deflect the question.

If it is unanswerable, try a variation on any of the following:

- 'You've raised an interesting point which would be too complex to answer in the limited time available. Perhaps you could seek me out at the end of the session, and we could discuss this area in detail.'
- 'I'd like to have a stab at answering that, but our expert in this area would be far better qualified. He/she will be joining us for drinks/at lunch; I will introduce you then.'
- 'I'd like to check on the background/one or two details before I answer that question. If you leave me your card, I will telephone you with an answer in the next couple of days.'

Add that any other member of the audience keen to have the question answered should also let you know of their interest at the end of the address. The chances are that any question you cannot answer is going to be complex and of little general interest, so you will have done the audience a favour by deflecting it.

Even if you should be expected to know the answer, don't be afraid of admitting that you do not know. Don't make it a sorry admission, merely a statement of fact. Your candour and straight talking will do you credit. Do make sure that you promise to find out the answer and let the questioner know.

If you are organising a speaking session, ensure that the individual chairing it is aware of these procedures. It is the Chairman's responsibility to shield a speaker who is getting into difficulties. He or she is entitled to break in with one of the deflection responses, if it is clear that the question is mischievous or tangential.

Using such an approach provides a safety net – and thus the security necessary to build confidence in one's talk.

Documentation

Do not hand out transcripts or notes at the beginning of the talk. This will merely lead to delegates reading rather than listening.

On arrival, each member of the audience should be given a running order, giving the bare bones of your talk. It should be made clear, perhaps by the chairman, that full notes will be given out at the end, but delegates should still be given paper and pen/pencil to note down key facts. A delegate list is a bonus.

As they leave, they can be given full information packs and any appropriate marketing material.

This information pack is the correct place for your accumulation of knowledge. The speech should enthuse delegates sufficiently to want to learn more. The notes should fill in most of the gaps. They should not, however, answer all questions, or you would be out of work. The well-crafted presentation and pack should drive delegates into the arms of the firm involved, having persuaded the client that you are the fount of wisdom and the right provider of advice and service.

In smaller gatherings

One of the things you cannot do in a conference is physically touch your audience. If you, now reading this paragraph, were asked whether you would want to touch members of the audience, the chances are low.

However, making physical contact, in a meeting for example, can make a substantial difference to how you are perceived. We would all shy away from anything demonstrative, but it may be worth illustrating the benefits that can accrue, by quoting Kim Tasso who relates what took place in a famous psychology experiment conducted in the US.

This 'involved a librarian checking out books to students. On the control trials, the librarian passed the books to the students without actually touching them, whereas on the experimental trials, the librarian acted in exactly the same manner, but managed to brush the students' hands lightly as the books were passed across. Outside the library, the students were asked a series of questions about the efficiency and friendliness of the librarian. The students who had been touched (although they were not aware of the contact) gave much higher scores'.

Similar contact when passing documents, a touch on someone's arm, or a guiding arm on the shoulder or back, are likely to draw a similarly positive, though unacknowledged, response. After all, none are any more intrusive than a handshake, itself merely a formalised acknowledgement of the importance of physical contact in demonstrating collaboration and friendliness.

A detailed examination of interpersonal behaviour in meetings would take up many pages and, diverting as it might be, would threaten to take the theme of this book into an abstract and peripheral grey area. Interested readers are encouraged to seek solace in the existing caucus of work available elsewhere. The power of controlled physicality in professional relationships is a fascinating but fraught field of study, particularly in view of the fact that, as has been pointed out to the author, 'behaviour such as this carries a jail sentence or death by stoning in some parts of the world'.

Summary

Key points

- In presentations, form is at least as important as content. Be interesting, not all-knowing.
- Keep it simple. Repeat core message(s) and sum up frequently.
- Rehearse – and keep rehearsing until you do not need to read your notes. Timing and rehearsal are everything in professional speaking.

Subsidiary points

- Shape all content so that it will appeal/be relevant to the audience.
- Use the active and involve the audience; talk about 'you' and 'we' rather than merely recount passive facts.
- Present information practically, not theoretically; ideally, it should be shaped into benefits rather than simply facts or features.
- Relegate detail to the handout notes.
- Enthuse. A presentation is an opportunity to sell yourself and your firm. Enthusiasm is catching and effective. Adopt passion rather than excess formality.
- Start with an explicit agenda and signpost your delivery. Tell people where you are in your talk, so that anyone who has lost the thread can pick it up again. Use question phrases such as 'So what have we established?' or 'Where does this take us?'.
- Repeat your central message. Say what you are going to say. Say it. Then say what you have just said.
- Use cue cards. These should contain key words only. Glance at these – don't read them.
- Paint pictures to enliven your text. However mundane, complex or dry the subject, it can be brightened by examples, anecdotes, similes, metaphors, idiomatic phrases etc.
- Use light humour – but never jokes demanding laughter.
- Use the full inflection of your voice. Start sentences on a high note and end them on a low one. Use stresses to punctuate your delivery.
- Maintain eye contact with the audience. Avoid looking at the ceiling and the floor.
- Be natural. Treat the audience as a friend. Forget that public speaking is an unnatural process and use the techniques given in this chapter to overlay a natural and conversational style.
- Use your body to endorse the message you are trying to convey. If

SPEAKING IN PUBLIC

you are talking about size, spread your arms; if passionate about a point, pound the table; if you are being derisory about someone's feeble reaction to legislation, act out their pusillanimous response. Body language is much more potent than words.

- Use whole arm gestures, rather than sharp twitching movements.
- Begin and end well. This is when audiences' attention is at its height.
- Pause. This paces your talk, gives you a chance to think and an air of authority.
- Use visual aids sparingly. They should illustrate facts or act as sign-posts; if they merely repeat what you are saying, drop them. Talk to the audience, not to your visual aids.
- Dress as you would for a client meeting.
- Deal with questions courteously. If you do not know the answer, do not bluster. Ask to take the question after the session, or promise to investigate the matter and revert by telephone.
- Practice. Only by rehearsing will you be sufficiently confident of your material to concentrate on the real purpose of the presentation: to win over the audience through your performance.

Hints and tips

- Bite the tip of your tongue lightly to induce a natural flow of saliva if your mouth dries.
- If you do not know what to do with your hands, hold cue cards with one, clasping the loose hand around the first. Alternatively, if you tend to sway, rest one hand or knuckle on a table. This will 'ground' you. The most natural way to hold your hands (though it does not feel natural) is by your sides.
- Learn and rehearse your opening half minute, so that you can per-form on autopilot if necessary. Once this is out of the way, you will have relaxed slightly and your brain will have begun to work again!
- Don't ever expect to rid yourself of nerves. Simply keeping them on your side (using adrenaline positively) should be the height of your ambitions. After a lifetime on the stage, many of the greatest actors are still ill with nerves before a performance.
- Use a radio microphone. It stops you having to worry about ampli-fication and allows you to move around (not, I stress, fidget around) if you have the inclination and confidence.
- Keep a clock visible. Make sure you do not overrun your allotted

124

7 Beauty parades and proposal documents

The human brain starts working the moment you are born and never stops until you stand up to speak in public.

Sir George Jessell

Many of the points pertinent to presentations in general apply to pitches for new business. However, there are additional factors to bear in mind.

The most obvious difference lies in a formal pitch's constraints. Content is dictated by a brief, and follows client priming in the form of a proposal document.

The proposal document

Creating and submitting a proposal is often a wearing process; the drafting has to be squeezed around fee earning or existing work, often against a series of constricting deadlines. With this in mind, it is important to establish and follow a tight structure.

There is no point in writing anything until the shape of the document has been outlined and agreed, and it is established who will be drafting what. It can take longer to work back from a false start than to start afresh.

John de Forte of de Forte Associates compares proposal creation to building a house, where, he suggests, 'you would presumably decide on the floor plan before you turned your attention to the lighting and decoration. The same applies when the edifice you are constructing is a proposal document. So begin with the floor plan, or synopsis'.

This needs to be done as a group. All those who will be involved in the drafting process should be present. Only then will each person understand the context of their contribution. If this does not happen, the document will take far longer – and will be more difficult to get right.

125

Once this meeting has established agreement on the approach, each member can map out a contribution in bullet point or synopsis format.

If there is no obvious candidate, part of this meeting's purpose will be to appoint an editor for the proposal document. This person is responsible for remaining in sight if the wood as well as the trees. The editor's job is often easiest if all contributions are received as bullet points rather than finished prose, in that he or she can then compile a full draft in a single homogenous style.

Constituent parts

Every pitch document will be different (though some are criminally alike). However, each is likely to comprise of:

- details of how the team's approach will meet the client's objectives;
- background on the team;
- information on how the project will be managed;
- fee levels and structures;
- credentials of the firm.

An executive summary may be added at the front of the document, and a covering letter will accompany the package. It is usual for this covering letter to consist of no more than a platitude or two and a reference to the proposal document itself; this is a waste. Since the letter is the first thing seen by the client, it should create an immediate and powerful impression. Make sure it contains succinct references to the differentiating points and key benefits of your pitch.

A good rule is to put your firm at the back of the document and your client at the front. Start by addressing the issues that they are facing, restricting references to yourself to instances where your activities will solve the client's problems. Celebrating your fitness for the task and your relevant experience should be left to the final section of the proposal.

Keep detailed descriptions of procedures to the minimum, unless wholly relevant to the management of the project and clearly communicable as client benefits. Major on the strength of your ideas and personnel. Remember that, to the client, the track record of the firm is secondary in importance to the calibre of the people who will work on their business. Make sure that sufficient attention is paid to this part of the document, and that those who feature here, and what is said, tallies with any presentation given to the potential client.

When putting together the constituent parts of the document, it is important to steer clear of self-serving puffery. Demonstrate experience through citing case histories; describe how benefits would be felt by the client, rather than weakly suggest that they will occur.

Having run through details of how work will be managed, be bullish about your fee structure. If your charges are low, make sure you appear cost-effective rather than cheap. If you command high fees, emphasise value for money and make no self-depreciating allusions. Stress fee-related positives, such as the practical steps you will take to control costs (monitoring, reporting, the judicious use of senior/junior staff resources). Show your long-term commitment and vision by alluding to future fee structures and reviews.

Finally, tailor your credentials to the client's likely interests not to the general strengths of your firm. The client is only concerned with your past, present and future performance in relevant fields. Seek quality copy here, not undigested and untargeted accounts of your achievements.

Packaging and delivery

A theme of this book is the equal or superior impact of appearance over content. Such a contention is, of course, provocative. In truth, each has different functions. Appearance wins attention; content retains or loses it. It follows, therefore, that excellent content can remain unnoticed unless properly presented.

It is illogical, in this light, to submit a proposal document that matches the quality of work contained, and alluded to, within its covers. Make sure that this is the case, and make equally sure that it reaches its destination. Have the proposal document hand-delivered and make absolutely certain that the intended recipient has taken possession of your submission.

If all goes to plan, you will be invited to attend a beauty parade. In this case, what makes the difference between success and failure in a pitch for new business? Often the answer lies in how benefits are conveyed to the potential client.

Which of these sentences would impress you most in a presentation?

- 'We have established an excellent reputation as advisers in your sector of the market. Though you have pointed out that we are more expensive than your existing lawyers, we are confident that we are cost-effective, and can save you money in the long run through speed and efficiency'.

Or simply

- 'We would expect to save you 5% on your existing overheads over the next 12 months'.

This is not intended to be a direct comparison - merely a demonstration that a single benefit is far superior to a series of features.

If we chose suppliers on content alone, there would be no need for pitches. Proposal documents would suffice. People buy people. Hence it is vital to perform appropriately in a pitch.

The brief

Check on the individual requirements of the brief. Make sure you respond specifically to each both in proposal and pitch.

If you are not offered the chance to be briefed in person, and are expected to respond to a piece of paper, ask to meet anyway. You can point out your belief that a successful working relationship must be built on the personalities involved and that you will only be able to get a 'feel' for the client's business by meeting.

At the brief, initially you should keep your ideas to yourself and your powder dry. The brief is a time to listen, the proposal, the place to expand and the presentation the time to speak.

This does not mean you should avoid questions at a briefing, merely that you should assimilate first.

There are many pitch losers who never asked for information necessary to fill gaps in their knowledge, thinking this to be an indication of weakness. If you are in doubt, ask, but only after you have taken in the full brief.

Research

Clients buy professional services because they need to solve a problem, exploit an opportunity, offload work elsewhere, comply with an obligation, gain advice, or gain third party support for an initiative. The most important first step when invited to tender for work is to find out which of the above apply.

Find out all you can about the company culture and the nature of the people to whom you will pitch. It is useful to talk to several people within the company, to determine whether they have a different angle on the problem you hope to solve. Note their phrases and terminology so that you can repeat these in the proposal. This will indicate to the client that you understand their industry.

Try to discover who you are pitching against. Never rubbish the opposition directly, but use this information to determine what you can offer that will be different from that likely to emanate from your rivals.

Establishing rapport

An obvious, essential yet often overlooked element in a business pitch is the establishment of a relationship with the potential client. Your excellent reputation or relevant experience may prove of secondary importance to 'I felt that we could work together', or 'We speak the same language.' You can leave this relationship-building to fate, or you can work on it.

Stephen Clues makes the point that establishing rapport is the very purpose of beauty parades. 'The place to demonstrate expertise,' he points out, 'is in the written proposal beforehand. In a pitch, the clients want to see who will be doing the work and how they work as a team.'

Keep it simple

Don't fall into the trap of spouting an oral version of your written proposal. Your spoken presentation should be simple and should concentrate on core points. Leave the details and ancillary facts to your document. Concentrate on meeting the objectives, explaining how you will personally approach the project (and how you feel about it) and the benefits of this approach.

Most unsuccessful beauty parade presentations fail because, like conference and seminar speeches, they try to cram in too much. The successful pitch takes the information which research shows to be most relevant to the client's needs, and presents it in the form of easily-understood benefits.

For example, 'Shuffle & Smith is a small firm (feature) which means the person you meet will also be controlling your affairs' (benefit). 'We are specialists in commercial law for small businesses (feature) so we are able to provide you with a single point of contact for all your business' legal needs' (benefit).

The prime benefit should arise from the result. 'Our input into your business will ensure that problems are eradicated at birth, not allowed to develop and threaten your continued success.'

All clients want to know what benefits you can provide for them. If any part of your presentation suggests no benefit to the client, drop it.

It is essential that benefits meet the brief. The Huthwaite Research Group investigated sales pitches in 23 countries, over a period of 12 years, analysing 35,000 encounters. They discovered that, in order to make a discernible difference, a true benefit must be conveyed to show how a product or service meets 'an explicit need which has been expressed by the customer' – the client. In other words, if a benefit merely shows how a service can be used, or can help the client, it has minimal impact.

Bear in mind when planning your pitch that the end goal for the client is always the same: a solution to their stated needs which brings reassurance and peace of mind.

A useful exercise is to reduce what you want to say to bare essentials. Then add examples, illustrations and, if appropriate, visual aids. Far too many beauty parades focus on dry fact, when what is needed is a lighter, more human approach. Anecdotes or examples which demonstrate your experience and expertise are worth hours of self-congratulation.

Remember that a presentation is *primarily* about selling yourself – not your firm, product or service. Vital as the latter are, you won't win the business unless you first win the client's respect for you personally.

Timing and length

Team presentations often consist of a seamless flow of information, leaving the client little opportunity to comment or ask questions. Sometimes presenters fear that questions will interrupt the presentation and can make it difficult to control the situation.

Try welcoming feedback. Build natural breaks into a pitch presentation, so that the client can respond. Use open questions to elicit a comment, such as 'How does this sound so far?' or 'Have any of you had personal experience of this?'

Of course, by allowing input from the client there is a risk that you may lose control if there is too much discussion. Therefore it is useful to summarise earlier points, before resuming where you left off.

Share a presentation evenly. It is a mistake to let the most senior presenter fire all the ammunition. The impression is left of an unbalanced team, dominated by someone the client may not see too often on the day to day work. Everyone should have an equal amount of information to impart. If this is not the case omit someone from the pitch or relocate. Someone with little or no role will embarrass the client as well as that individual.

Equally important, make sure you direct your message to all of those in the room. If you aim all your best shots at the most senior person present, you will alienate his or her colleagues. Ensure you distribute your eye contact evenly.

Patience and practice

There is no substitute for thorough preparation and rehearsal. Many people feel awkward about practising without an audience. However, rehearsals are worthwhile, especially for team presentations. If you can rope in a few colleagues to act as the client it will be more realistic. Always time your practice sessions and decide how you will hand over between presenters.

Also determine whether you will each introduce yourselves with a mini-biography before presenting the proposal. This saves the other presenter(s) from feeling redundant if they are the last to speak.

In the actual presentation, when answering questions, avoid discussing each point in too much detail. Give short succinct answers and keep moving the discussion forward.

When your perfectly reasonable proposals are met by provocative comments, continue to be patient and reasonable. In beauty parades, the client team will inevitably feature someone whose job it is to shoot holes in your presentation. Never take issue or argue, no matter how confontational the stance taken.

If you practice adequately, you will appear to be in complete control of your material. Rehearsal will bring a natural and confident quality to what might otherwise be a stiffly formal presentation. Mark Twain made the point clearly, when he said 'it usually takes me more than three weeks to prepare a good impromptu speech'.

Be human!

Nerves can cause us to project an image which is misinterpreted. Remember you are presenting to another human being. Smile. A client is more likely to choose a friendly face than one which is stuck in a superior sneer or deep frown.

Above all, as in any presentation, meet your listeners' eyes. You will not appear credible or trustworthy, whatever your track record, if you give your presentation looking at the ceiling or at your notes. Avoid fiddling with pens, rings or clothing. It is a distraction and a dead give-away that you're feeling anxious.

Keep your voice level up and avoid letting it drop at the end of sentences. Convey enthusiasm. Even the most cynical of listeners will take some pride in his or her organisation. It is important that you show how keen you are to work with this client. Superior ennui does not win business.

You can be extremely knowledgeable and still be friendly. Help the client to like you so that they find it easy to work with you.

Since a good presentation and a bad one can represent the difference between success and failure, it seems foolish to put days of work into written documents and then try to 'busk' the pitch. It is the latter which will sell you as an individual and as a firm; the proposal may get you the opportunity to present and then determine whether you are viable in terms of track record, price and so forth, but it is the pitch which will win hearts and minds.

Summary

- In an oral brief, listen. Leave most of the talking to the presentation.
- Arrange to meet the client to discuss elements of a written brief and to research the client's needs.
- Research the organisation, its people and its requirements.
- Find out with whom you are competing and differentiate yourself.
- Appoint someone to coordinate proposal production.
- Allocate roles for document submissions and pitch speaking slots.
- Ensure that the document addresses client problems and your solutions.
- Make sure your proposal looks good and gets delivered to the right person in the right place at the right time.
- Practice the presentation, alone and as a team.
- Keep the presentation simple and focus on the client's key objectives. Address the brief in all respects, but refer the audience to the pitch documentation for detail.
- Avoid using legal jargon.
- Convey benefits, not features. Focus on how you can provide solutions to problems.
- Perform, don't just talk. Convey personality, not mere knowledge.
- Encourage feedback during a presentation.
- Share the presentation equally between speakers.
- Establish and maintain eye contact.
- Show enthusiasm and interest.
- Leave all extraneous detail to the pitch documentation.

Hints and tips

- Remember and use the names of those to whom you are presenting.
- Use the jargon contained in the client's briefing documents.
- Address all members of the panel, not just the most senior.
- Take risks; don't sit on the fence.
- Integrate the handling of difficult questions when doing your dress rehearsal.
- Keep the use of audio visual aids to a minimum. A flip chart is adequate. Slides or acetates can look over-slick and require dimmed lights.

8 Crisis management

There cannot be a crisis next week. My schedule is already full.

Henry Kissinger

What is crisis management?

A brief definition might capture it as 'planning to prevent problems becoming public relations nightmares'.

Crisis management establishes contingency plans to ensure control of the communication process, when rumour and media interest threaten to wrest that control from an organisation. It is an irrelevance to those who hold the view that 'it couldn't happen here' or 'we would just say 'no comment'.

Yet every professional firm should have a crisis management plan. The alternative is to let neutral or negative rumours develop into damning 'facts'.

If you do not have a voice in a debate, then the contrary view will triumph. Crisis management is about ensuring that a firm has a voice.

What is a crisis?

Overreacting to an anodyne enquiry might imply problems where none occur. So when do you let problems wilt naturally and when do you nip them in the bud?

A simple definition of a crisis might be any situation where negative publicity is more than just a faint possibility. For example, a disgruntled client is known to have talked to the press; you are being sued for negligence; or a member of staff has committed a criminal offence. Equally, contingency plans might accompany any controversial aspect of business, relating to a client's activities, your decision to sack staff, take over a competitor or relocate.

The most bland of developments can blow up into a problem. An incident involving a tea lady unexpectedly splashed one law firm across the tabloids. Like a car crash, a crisis may not be your fault, may happen without warning, and may be fatal. Every firm must have a crisis management plan. The vital first requirement is anticipation.

Preparing people

The firm needs to have a crisis management committee, to whom all partners should report any potential accidents waiting to happen. Ideally, this should include the senior partner, managing partner and whoever is responsible for public (specifically media) relations. Since crises, by definition, usually occur suddenly and require swift and authoritative responses, usual communication channels need to be overridden and clear, short lines of communication established.

As soon as a development occurs that threatens to affect the good name of the firm, the team should meet to prepare a contingency response. Obviously circumstance will dictate the exact nature of the response, but the following will usually be necessary:

- Determine the true nature of the situation. Issue a preliminary (holding) statement, if the facts are not immediately apparent.
- Prepare a statement when all pertinent information is known. This should present the facts according to the firm. The statement should be dated and a time of release noted.
- Decide who should take the spokesperson's role.
- Ensure that reception and switchboard direct any press enquiries to the team.
- Issue the statement, with a memorandum to all partners in all offices, alerting them to the situation, reminding them to treat enquiries courteously but to refer them to the statement/spokesperson.
- It is not always necessary or advisable to notify all staff, simply because this may feed the rumour mill. However, if a negative story is going to be broadcast widely, then it is sensible and indicative of good internal communications to arm your staff with your version of the story.
- It is wise for someone to keep a record of events, particularly if the problem is sufficiently serious that it is likely to snowball. This should record the time, nature and content of every call received or made. Such an account might prove invaluable in countering or correcting the sort of inaccuracies that can arise.

Statements and no comment

The statement is a vital tool. It ensures that a considered, defensible and consistent view is publicised. It prevents having to make off-the-cuff oral comments, which can easily be twisted. It also averts the possibility of a 'no comment'.

Saying 'no comment' is a simple, tempting course of action – or inaction. It is also, almost always, a disastrous choice. It conveys guilt, or at the very least an image of defensiveness or insouciance.

A statement may have very little to say, but it is superior to 'no comment' every time. It indicates a readiness to respond and gives the issuer a chance to say something. Even if that something is insubstantial, the statement will be reproduced by any responsible publication, lending a potentially positive gloss to what may be an otherwise negative slant. Why settle for 'no comment' – a response which endorses such negativity?

Think about the last time you heard or read about a news story, where a spokesperson or woman said 'no comment', or 'was unavailable for comment'. The media, frustrated in their natural hunt for feedback, feel unsurprisingly aggrieved when faced by a brick wall. Thus they will recount your lack of comment in such a way that you will seem to have something to hide.

The statement should be produced on headed paper or press release paper. It should have a brief underlined heading, under the word 'statement'. The first paragraph should give a resume of the facts followed by the firm's position and any clarification deemed necessary.

In other words, a statement is not a press release and does not follow press release rules. You are not looking to attract attention, but to show understanding and mastery of a situation.

The tone should be measured, assured and rational. No one should be attacked or ridiculed. Complaints, defensiveness or sardonic asides should be excised from any draft.

The remainder of the statement should add any additional pertinent information. However, brevity should be pursued wherever possible.

The extension number should be given for the room in which the spokesperson can be found, along with his or her home number and a fax number for incoming enquiries. Add any mobile phone or pager numbers that may be of use to a journalist. It is vital that you speak to anyone writing an article, simply to ensure that your voice is heard. As already intimated, being 'unavailable for comment' is only marginally better than 'declined to comment'.

If the crisis is of major proportions, the team dealing with it should congregate in a single room, with a telephone and word processor, and with a secretary constantly present. Ideally, there should also be a fax and mobile telephone in the room.

CRISIS MANAGEMENT

Rehearsing and preparing for a crisis can make the difference between a measured response and fanning the flames. Adequate preparation means that everything follows defined courses – from briefed people following defined actions to address labels being prepared in advance.

Responding to calls

If a journalist calls with an aggressive line of questioning, calm, confident replies will do more to convey probity than angry denials. An obvious point, perhaps, on paper, but one easily forgotten in the heat of an attack on a firm's reputation.

As calls are received, the spokesperson should try to find from each journalist what they have heard. This may affect the nature of the statement. It is essential to establish the name, telephone number and publication/broadcaster for whom the journalist is working.

Answers to specific questions should be courteous, but should add nothing to the official statement. If you are thrown by a question, ask to have it restated. If a journalist makes an incorrect assumption before leading on to a question, challenge and correct the assumption.

There is no reason why you have to answer anything immediately; ask to call the individual back in five minutes, if you need to consult over an unexpected line of questioning.

Similarly, if a journalist is writing an in-depth article, ask to have a list of questions faxed to you. Find out the deadline for a response and make sure you meet it with a written response.

Ask for a fax number to which the official statement should be sent.

A conversation on the telephone, in the heat of a crisis, has much in common with giving a presentation. There is a tendency to speed up, to gabble, to lose control. As in a presentation, introduce an artificial slowness to your delivery, and use the pause. This will give you the chance to order your thoughts, while simultaneously creating an impression of calm and control.

Taking the initiative

If a situation requires you to initiate contact with the media, the fastest way is to fax your statement or document to one of the commercial agencies who specialise in circulating urgent documents to the media.

The Press Association, for example, will do this free if they think you have a newsworthy story; agencies such as Two Ten Communications will issue any material you wish to have circulated to an agreed list of recipients, for a fee.

Your PR office or consultancy will be able to advise you on the detail, but usually the choice of recipients is made by reading or faxing codes taken from a media manual, relating to all those publications you want notified. The agency is then able to use its multifax facility, or send text 'down the line' by wire, straight to the screens of the newsroom.

RESPONDING TO A CRISIS: KEY STEPS

INFORMATION RECEIVED	CRISIS COMMITTEE MEETS MONITOR PRESS/OTHER CONTACT RECORD ALL CONTACTS	GATHER INFORMATION	DRAFT STATEMENT	DISSEMINATE INFORMATION INTERNALLY	DISSEMINATE INFORMATION EXTERNALLY	UPDATE OR REVISE STATEMENT AS NECESSARY
INFORM ALWAYS	Switchboard & Reception to route all calls to Meeting			Partners involved Fee Earners & Staff	Press Enquirers Client Enquirers	
INFORM IF APPROPRIATE				Other (uninvolved) Staff	Key Media Clients	All those who saw original statement, if facts have changed

Fig 18

If you have your own multifax, it is worth considering (as part of the crisis management pre-preparation process) whether to have available pre-addressed fax cover sheets to key press contacts. Thus you would be able to issue a statement, if circumstances demanded, within seconds of having it printed out.

If you do not have a means of logging media coverage, arrange this either via any on-line data-gathering facilities you have in your library or IT department, or via a specialist press cuttings agency. The latter will need a brief as to what they should look out for, and which press sectors they should monitor. If you wish to check for TV or radio mentions, you will need to do this through a specialist broadcast monitoring organisation.

Other enquiries

Not all enquiries will come from the press. If a problem turns into media coverage, calls will come in from all sides – from the client, to competitors, to the car company you use. Depending on the nature of the trouble, you may receive calls from an MP's office, the Law Society, or from other regulatory or trade bodies.

In all cases, much can be gained by being helpful, noting requirements, and responding as openly as possible. Ensure that the statement continues to be used and is updated if necessary (in which case it may need to be selectively reissued). Indicate the speed at which you are working to put matters/rumours right, the seriousness with which you view allegations, the fact that the client's business remains unaffected. Upbeat, positive messages without ignoring or downplaying problems will satisfy most enquirers.

In some cases, you may need to pre-empt client concerns by sending the statement and a covering letter to those clients likely to be particularly affected or concerned by negative publicity. Doing this by fax is a swift option, though the lack of security involved may be a factor militating against such a course of action.

It is advisable to subcontract this job to partners from each department, who should submit their list of recipients to the crisis management team (to avoid duplications) and then orchestrate mailing or faxing.

The silver lining

An organisation that keeps its head in a crisis can turn attention in its favour. All publicity is not good publicity, but most presents an opportunity.

If you have nothing to hide, invite the media to visit your offices. Meeting face to face can build trust where previously there had been only suspicion. Don't let this trust go to your head – you can never guarantee that 'off the record' promises will be honoured. However, do take the chance to build a relationship and, importantly, convey good things about your firm.

If you have suffered negative publicity, the temptation is to keep a low profile. Sometimes this may be the best course of action, but consider whether you should not be taking steps to balance the bad press you have endured. Perhaps you should follow up the attention you have had by inviting journalists to see 'the other side' of your firm. If your profile is inadvertently high, this provides a level of interest in you which can be capitalised upon, rather than bewailed.

An awareness of the need to plan for crises can rub off on clients. Having communicated the need for crisis management to key clients, Ince & Co have found their name and number emblazoned on clients' emergency response cards.

The crisis management exercise

When a crisis breaks, it is unlikely that you will reach for this book and urge your fellows to follow its precepts. Even were you to do so, it is likely that you would be preaching to headless chickens. However calm we may imagine ourselves in a crisis, most people fail to perform to their full potential when under stress.

Firms have fire drills to familiarise people with the layout of the building, the location of fire exits and the correct course of action. The same rationale applies to crisis drills.

There is no substitute in learning to deal with a crisis than running a monitored exercise. This entails a scenario being worked up and unleashed on the crisis management team. The level of sophistication might run from a single trainer-monitor verbally introducing hypothetical events, to the employment of actors and television crews to enact pre-planned activities.

Such an exercise requires a suspension of disbelief from the protagonists. It should be run, and treated, as a genuine crisis. It should be planned in such a way that responses can be anticipated and different results to the firm's statements and actions can be introduced and developed. A period of weeks can be concentrated artificially into the day or days of the exercise.

With proper pre-planning, the evolving nature of a news story can be depicted dramatically. Mocked up copies of *The Lawyer*, carrying a small story might be followed by dummies of *The Times*, examining a related issue. This might lead to the next week's issue of *The Lawyer* carrying a front page lead and editorial.

Depending on the nature of the problem, any number of possibilities might arise. For example, trade magazines might begin to pick up

CRISIS MANAGEMENT

on the publicity. Clients would begin calling. Rumours would start to fly around the firm. Inaccurate quotes might begin to feature in unsubstantiated reporting. TV cameras might arrive in the building, hidden in the bags of pushy investigative journalists. The tabloids might run a scare story about arrogant law firms oppressing impoverished clients.

Until such a hypothetical exercise is conducted, you will never know how well or badly your firm would handle a crisis. Monitoring the exercise, reporting the findings, and re-running a (new) scenario, are all vital elements towards ensuring that, if a genuine crisis arose, your team would respond effectively.

Summary

- Produce a crisis management plan and conduct a crisis handling exercise. Only then will you be in a position to handle the real thing.
- When a crisis breaks, inform the members of the crisis committee. If there isn't one, ensure that the senior and managing partners are informed.
- Designate a room and telephone line exclusively to deal with the crisis.
- Gather the facts.
- Prepare and issue a statement. This should be factual, non-defensive or censorious, authoritative and succinct.
- Appoint an official spokesperson.
- Brief all those within the firm likely to be effected. This includes all partners.
- Circulate the statement internally (to all staff) if it is known that a contrary view is being published or broadcast. Ensure that staff are your allies not your opposition.
- Ensure that switchboard and reception are briefed and instructed to route all relevant enquiries to the crisis committee.
- Deal with all enquiries courteously. Stick to the statement. Avoid 'no comment' responses. If uncertain as to a reply, take the caller's details and say you will respond after a period of internal consultation.
- Find out as much as you can about each caller. Record telephone, fax and address details. Ensure every caller has a copy of the statement. If a journalist has a deadline, make sure you meet it.
- Keep a record of all actions, calls and responses.
- Circulate the statement to press unprompted, and to clients, if the crisis demands preventative steps, or if a story needs to be countered or contained.
- Follow up poor publicity by inviting the media to see/hear the other side of the story.
- Be positive, helpful and approachable at all times, however annoying the behaviour of others may be.

9 Corporate hospitality and sponsorship

When the professional advisers first descended on the legal world, it was fashionable to decry corporate hospitality (or corporate entertainment) as outdated, irrelevant, expensive and redundant.

This was (a) absurd and (b) foolish. Lawyers like to entertain and be entertained. Even if unjustifiable as promotional activity (though this is not the case), attending the races, the opera or a good restaurant are important perks of the job. No lawyer is going to listen to a jumped up marketeer pour scorn on activities which both please and build relationships.

Even if not consciously seen as promotional activities, such corporate hospitality formed and still contributes much of the oil which lubricates the wheels of client relationships and hence progress.

That said, corporate entertainment also has a defined role and a part to play in the planned approach to marketing activity. Elevating it from the personal to the general takes it from a largely invisible aspect of practice development to an important and systematic place in the promotion of a law firm.

According to Fig 19 (p 138), entertainment alone (ie without sponsorship) recently accounted for the largest slice of the promotional pie.

The rationale

Corporate hospitality does not only generate goodwill. A well chosen event provides an opportunity for lawyer and guest to discuss business matters in a relaxed and amicable environment. Future plans, competitor activities and other background can be filled in. Intentions can be gauged and opportunities explored without pressures of time or a business ambience.

Thus corporate hospitality should continue to form part of the promotional mix. The question is how.

HOW LAW FIRMS DIVIDE PROMOTIONAL SPEND (%)

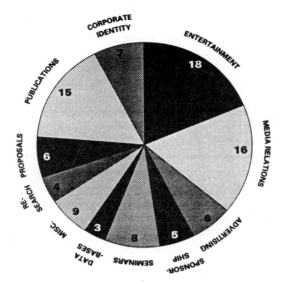

Fig 19

The approach

A fully functioning database can make the process quasi-scientific. Systems can be set up to prompt a firm when contacts x, y and z have not used the firm for a period of time and should be met. Alternatively, client interests can be logged and those keen on tennis invited to Wimbledon, those keen on horses to a race meeting and those keen on music to a concert.

A more piecemeal but realistic approach (who has the time and expertise to monitor the database adequately and then activate programmes?) is to invite all favoured, important and other key contacts to an event or events staged or supported by the firm. This has the advantage of being relatively easy to arrange. It provides a clear focus on the firm as an entity and allows all partners and fee earners to put on a show of strength.

This can be arranged incidentally, taking advantage of a sporting or artistic event, or it can be arranged through sponsorship.

The sponsorship route

Corporate entertainment is a subject in itself, but is also often an adjunct of sponsorship. Once thought of as simply name-association, sponsorship is now a sophisticated field, with all of the complexities, irrelevancies, opportunities and costs that the word 'sophistication' usually hides or implies.

If you decided to sponsor European golf for example, you would probably find yourself entrenched in negotiations with a range of conflicting bodies, discussing co-sponsor status in different countries, and being sold packages on the basis of camera coverage of your logo (referred to as 'opportunities to see' by the salesman). Quite apart from the unlikelihood of such a sponsorship being appropriate, it is unlikely to appeal or make sense financially. However, one element would almost certainly appeal – the corporate hospitality aspect.

Here you would be offered free passes for yourself and your clients to the main events, VIP status in your own tent, receptions with the golfing stars, chauffeur links between hotel and course, silver service lunches – and so on.

Suddenly sponsorship sounds more attractive. Often this is for the wrong reason – the immediate personal appeal of the above. However, it may be that it is the direct link to the client's interest that has captured your imagination. If this is the case, the exercise is worth exploring further. If corporate entertainment can justify the cost of the sponsorship, the latter may prove a worthwhile and correct vehicle.

This is contrary to received sponsorship wisdom, where corporate hospitality is often but a small part of commercial sponsorship. It may be all but incidental, paling beside name awareness, branding rights and the like. However, to the law firm, it is almost certainly the main reason why a sponsorship may be undertaken, alongside the need to raise awareness of the firm in a market.

As always in a promotional event, it is essential to know who you hope to reach, before initiating activity. If a general message needs to be propagated to a large group (eg 'we are a firm of corporate finance specialists'), then raising and widening name awareness is probably the most important goal. You need a sponsorship which plasters your message high, far and wide. If, however, you need to convey a specific idea to a small group (eg 'we do more asset finance work than any other local firm') then you need to find a sponsorship vehicle that allows you to meet, entertain and impress the few key local people likely to respond to what you have on offer.

In such a case, where the target audience is comprised of a few, high profile decision-makers, corporate entertainment can reach people in ways that most promotional activities cannot.

Whether we like it or not (and most of us do like it), decisions rarely come from the facts and figures alone. They are just as likely to be effected via the building of mutual understanding and friendly relations in the theatre, on a tennis court or in a good restaurant.

Exploitation

If the package on offer looks interesting, do not buy it and then stop at that. Most sponsorship experts recommend spending the same amount of money as was invested in the sponsorship itself, in order to exploit the sponsorship opportunities. These include conducting client mailings, a media relations campaign to publicise aspects of your involvement, arranging staff incentives, possibly advertising your commitment – and, of course, arranging those added-value client entertainment aspects.

The impact of sponsorship may be subtle, but a failure to exploit it shrewdly would be wrong. Sponsorship is not about altruism. That is patronage. If you become involved in sponsorship, however worthy the cause, treat it as a commercial venture. You need to receive back as much as, or more than, you put in. Money that buys the sponsorship needs to buy promotional benefits, and additional money needs to be committed to reap the full potential rewards.

When negotiating a sponsorship, ensure that you gain a written record of what you are entitled to. If you merit three mentions in the programme and a logo on the invitations, determine exactly where and what size they will be. If you are entitled to a copy of a guest list, ascertain whether this includes invitees who do not attend and whether you can have the list on disk. It needs to be clear well in advance whether your senior partner will present a prize or merely sit at the top table. If your stand can be set up in an ante room, to endorse your sponsorship status, precise locations and dimensions need to be agreed.

Once again, it is advance consideration, lateral and logical thinking, plus careful planning which make sponsorship events succeed.

Building community relations

Sponsorship and patronage are distinct concepts, as has been mentioned, but they share common strands. Firms should consider whether patronage should not, in some cases, give way to sponsorship.

In many instances, it cannot and should not. However, when money is required by an organisation, sponsorship can often prove to be a mutually beneficial means of raising cash while providing a quid pro quo service to the donor in return.

A local initiative, whether it be the building of a hospital, supporting the rugby club or clearing the clogged canal, offers opportunities for a firm to show that it is part of the community.

Why bother?

Putting aside altruism, community sponsorship serves to expand local business links, raise profile and create goodwill. It associates law firms, which have a poor image in general, with 'putting something back'. Firms are often seen as distant, austere entities, seated in ivory towers and manned by the overpaid. Involvement in worthwhile initiatives can do much to right the balance, conveying contrary images to counter such negative perceptions.

What can be sponsored?

Anything. The obvious candidates are sporting, cultural and community-based activities. However, anything that needs financial help to get off the ground can be sponsored.

There is room for the imaginative firm to create sponsorships, rather than wait for the right one to arrive. If a firm knows that it needs to reach Australians working in the UK, for example, it could investigate sponsorship of the fixture between Australia and the local county cricket side, or, alternatively, it could suggest a sponsored issue of one of the Australian news publications produced in the UK. By creating a new idea, one can expect more control at less cost.

Television sponsorship, like advertising, entails a high cost, in return for a wide but poorly targeted reach. The high cost and poor targeting can be overcome by judicious choice. A regional firm with a strong agricultural practice could underwrite a specialist local farming programme at low cost and high impact.

The message in a sponsorship is subtler than in advertising, but gains from a form of editorial 'endorsement'. In other words, TV sponsorship connects the sponsor with the programme, rather than the overtly promotional commercial breaks.

The power, therefore, lies wholly in association. If the sponsorship is to work, the connotations of the programme must be wholly positive to the sponsor.

Other subjects

Additional common vehicles for sponsorship include competitions and awards. These work well when operated in tandem with a media relations campaign. Several firms have run prize competitions via national and regional newspapers, achieving prominence during the lifetime of the event.

A popular and obvious area where financial support has been traded in return for publicity is that occupied by exhibition, conferences and seminars. Such sponsorship opportunities can elevate a firm and its partners to a position of high visibility, without having to initiate bespoke events.

Similarly, a university, business school or other institution may seek help in funding a 'chair', course or wing. If you as a firm know who you want to reach, it is fairly easy to ascertain whether supporting such ventures is likely to reach that defined audience and thus make it worth your while offering the funding.

So what do you do when a senior partner tells you that it is a fine idea to sponsor the new library at his old college, to no obvious benefit? Tell him that this is patronage, not sponsorship? Refer him to the business plan?

There is, of course, no easy way out of this dilemma. However, the best approach is to steer the conversation round to the importance – to the firm, of course – of ensuring that the support offered brings about all the agreed requirements of a successful sponsorship. Produce the checklist at the end of this chapter and add a few disingenuous comments of surprise as you search for a single positive reason to proceed.

You may then find yourself looking for a new role in life, but you will be able to enjoy the warming conviction that you did the right thing.

Sponsorship agencies

For most sponsorships, you will not need an intermediary. For anything substantial, you probably do. The specialist will be able to find an appropriate sponsorship for you, broker a deal, advise on how best to exploit it, and then monitor the results. This may be in terms of media coverage or through interviews with those involved.

Summary

All sponsorships must:

- Conform to the general objectives set by business, marketing and promotional plans.
- Meet specific objectives.
- Reach a defined audience.
- Have specific, stipulated benefits.
- Have strong internal support within the firm.
- Be with an organisation whose staff appear competent and who distinguish clearly between your and their duties in the sponsorship.
- Have a timetable against which you can check that your objectives have been met and all agreed activities conducted.
- Give sufficient 'lead-time' to ensure that it is fully exploited.
- Have funds available to both run and develop it.
- Lend only positive connotations to the firm.
- Offer appropriate opportunities for client entertainment.
- Be long term and sustainable.
- Have some means of being assessed after the event, to check on whether success has been achieved.

The sponsorship may:

- Include rights to incorporation in the event title.
- Create media relations opportunities.
- Tie in with internal activities (entertainment, employee benefits or team-building).
- Suggest themes for an advertising campaign.
- Require a joint logo/press paper to be produced.

Checklist: to what are you entitled?

Branding

- How and where will the firm's name and logo appear?
- How and where will you be able to promote any secondary message you need to convey?
- What size limits/proportions will be imposed on your text and logo?
- Which other sponsors are involved? How will their names appear in relation to yours?

Corporate entertainment

- How many people will be given free tickets/can be entertained?
- How many will have special status?
- What does this entail?
- What transport/accommodation arrangements will be laid on?
- Will there be a chance to introduce VIP guests to royalty/celebrities?
- What food and drink will be served?
- Are the guests entitled to any other special privileges?
- When and how should guests be invited?

Publicity material

- Can you display your stand?
- Which/how many of the firm's publications can be distributed, and how?
- Can you circulate information in delegate wallets/visitor information?
- Are you entitled to free advertising in the event brochure?
- What form of editorial acknowledgement of your sponsorship contribution will there be in the official brochure?

Merchandising (umbrellas, gifts, etc)

- If produced, will your logo be included?
- Can merchandising be produced in your corporate colours?
- Are you entitled to a free supply?

10 Database

Lawyers are marvellous at keeping records. Every conversation is noted and filed in memorandum form. Client business can be traced back for decades.

Such skills have been necessitated by the demands of the job. Keeping equally good marketing records is a relatively new requirement. Many firms have grasped an opportunity. Others make do with mailing lists.

A mailing list is not a database list. The former is either a list kept on a word processor or a borrowed or bought hard copy. It can be amended, cut or added to, but otherwise it is inflexible.

A database, on the other hand, can do whatever it is asked to do. It is compiled and controlled using software that can order data in response to specific needs. It is set up so that each entry is coded, under different 'fields'. These codes mean that operators can draw off and recompile information based on specific criteria – such as geographical location, nature of main business, or attendance at a recent event.

A stand alone marketing database will do just this and nothing more. Integrated databases are of far greater use to the marketing function, in that they link into accounting or other electronic data. This means that they can be used to compile and produce high grade management information. Such a database could be said to be essential for any firm which really wants to know itself. As Don Moorhouse observes, 'how else can I, as the person responsible for managing my firm, really know how the firm's clients behave?'

With vast potential, there is a risk that users will want to direct such potential in different ways. Tesco offers the following illustration:

TO: IT Department
FROM: Senior Partner
SUBJECT: Marketing Database

My requirements are:
- Everybody to be able to update the information so we encourage greater use.

153

- The most basic information so that all contacts and clients are entered.
- The ability for lots of people to be associated with each client or contact to avoid 'that's my client' arguments.
- A really easy to use system.
- A simple, stand alone system.
- The ability for everyone to produce labels and letters.
- Reports that fit in my filofax.
- The ability to do my Christmas card list easily.
- A working system next week!

TO: IT Department
FROM: Managing Partner
SUBJECT: Marketing Database

My requirements are:
- Central updating for security, accuracy and control reasons.
- Basic information plus business sector interests, to allow careful targeting.
- One person to 'own' each client or contact to ensure someone is responsible for updating.
- A system with lots of functions and options.
- A system fully integrated with accounts, billing, etc.
- Central mailshots to avoid poor quality mailings and overmailing of certain clients.
- Reports that show all the information about each client.
- The ability to do a full blown client profitability and segmentation analysis.
- A working system next week!

A database can analyse industry sectors. It can be used to monitor contact with individual clients, indicate when records were updated, track referral of client work within the firm and assess how client organisations and their subsidiaries are related. Links to billing and accounting information allows analysis of client profitability, any relationship between income and any particular practice development initiative, and which of the firm's services have been used.

The disadvantage of such a database is perhaps obvious. It is a monumental task to set up and a horror to keep running. If insufficient time and resources are promised when embarking on such a venture, stop immediately.

Back then, for the moment, to the stand alone database, used primarily to support promotional work. Imagine that your firm is planning a seminar on the implications to property developers of new environmental legislation. You want to run this in the North of England, the Midlands, and the South.

Organising such a seminar, using mailing lists, might entail the following:

- Going through all records manually, to tick off intended invitees.
- Retyping the tick list into a bespoke seminar invitation list.
- Checking for duplications.
- Circulating the new list for final checking.
- Resolving disputes between partners about who should and who should not be invited, and by whom.
- Checking that changes of details not recorded on source lists are added to this new list.
- Deleting any previous list that might become confused with the new list.
- Pacifying partners when it becomes clear that their favoured clients have not received information.

How might this become less problematic?

If every list were loaded onto the database, checked once for duplications and errors, then life would, in theory, become far easier. In the example above, a database might allow the operator to pull out entries for clients and contacts on the basis of:

- Nature of business, to select property developers and associated professionals.
- Areas of interest, to find those who have shown past interest in environmental matters.
- Their geographical location, to determine to which seminar they should be invited.

Appropriate database systems allow each entry as much information as can usefully be stored. Thus, fields can be created for a range of categories, and records can be kept of all forms of contact.

The result should be a single centralised system on which all marketing records can be kept. As a way of monitoring client contact, it has no parallel. As a means of controlling efficient mailings, it can become indispensable to any firm.

Thus, the problems associated above with mailing lists should dissolve when using a database. If the database has been constructed properly, ie with the right instruction 'codes' against each entry, then the operator can pull off information as needed for any activity.

Changes are made to the central records, not to satellite lists. Therefore, because each client has only one listing, there is no need to cross-reference updated information. Clients invited to the environmental seminar would have this information automatically added to their records.

By linking the database to word-processing software, a word processed form letter can be 'mailmerged' with data held on the database. In other words, the computer cuts data from the database and pastes it into the body of the letter. This personalises the addresses, appellations, and even the text itself. It's a trick mastered years ago by the consumer marketeers.

Think of the letters you receive from insurance companies, *Reader's Digest*, indeed from all those who manage to send out literally millions of letters simultaneously, but who manage to insert your name miraculously into the third paragraph of your letter.

Marketing records

Bear in mind that list management and mailings are but one small aspect of a database. The potential is enormous. Depending on the amount of memory bought and the software's architecture, there is almost infinite capacity to hold and manipulate records. As mentioned, marketing lists and records can be linked with accounting and credit control functions. All client records can thus be recorded and ordered within a single electronic system.

An analogy would be a room full of filing cabinets. One holds records of work codes. Another has credit information in one draw and work in progress in another. A third cabinet is full of mailing lists. A fourth holds lists of the firm's clients by client partner – but also by SIC (Standard Industry Classification) code.

Thus all the information that the firm has on its clients and client records can be found in the room. But none of it interacts. None of it is linked.

A database is supposed to overcome the problem. It acts as a room full of filing records. Instead of hand searching for information, the database responds to typed in requests to provide and/or link together information.

For example. A command could be entered, asking to see a list of all clients looked after by Partners ABC and FGH who billed less than £5,000 during 1994.

To the marketeer, this information is invaluable. The greatest enemy of a firm is ignorance of its clients. The marketing functions of a database provide the solid information necessary to combat that ignorance, as well as a means of recording and monitoring initiatives taken to redress any perceived problems.

Anyone who has tried to create the brave new world of a database will recognise that this is largely rose tinted theory. In reality, database creation requires blood, sweat, tears, patience and long-term commitment.

When considering acquiring software and the hardware on which to run it, it is vital to invest in adequate expert consultancy and training. Only then will the venture have a chance of success, and of overcoming the resistance that will inevitably arise.

Objections

The following are among the most common reservations aimed at those who champion the idea of the electronic recording of client details on a database.

A database only works if its operator enters information correctly and it is kept up to date

This objection is valid, but palls insofar as the same applies to inferior mailing lists, which take far more time, over time, to run effectively.

They are expensive

This can be a fair point. The database software may not be prohibitively expensive, but it has to run on a mainframe. You may want to integrate database, word-processing, accounting and other record keeping within a combined system, so this may entail new computing structures and equipment. Then there is the time and cost required to move over from various lists to the new system, allowing for training, teething trouble and familiarisation.

Yet despite the short term costs and hiatus, the medium term should see tremendous benefits in terms of accuracy, efficiency and fringe benefits (new and informative reporting formats, long term morale and timesaving).

They serve no real purpose beyond mailings

In fact, in addition to providing useful management information, the centralised recording system allows a new perspective. No longer are client lists a threat and a problem. They are under control, easily organised and interpreted. This means that they can be used more effectively.

For example, it becomes easy to check that the right people are receiving the firm's publications. Responses to mailings, or other marketing events can be recorded. Instead of filing and losing that letter saying 'please let me know of any other events you have in my area', the database can be updated with this information and left to prompt the operator when asked who might be interested in a forthcoming event.

You may decide to contact all clients who have made their wills with you, after every budget. Instead of holding a bulging file of responses to previous mailings, comments made at meetings and suggestions from fee earners, you can centralise information on the database and personalise future mailings accordingly.

Importantly, if someone is doing some work for a client who is usually looked after by another partner, and discovers new or updated information on this person, he or she need notify only one person: the database operator. It would then be this person's responsibility to double check, with the client if appropriate, and with the client partner noted on the database. Once checked and amended, new facts are engraved into the system and errors could not be perpetuated.

Using an alternative to a central database, you are likely to find incorrect information being retained within a firm for years. However, this is apparently the norm, not the exception. According to The Robson Rhodes Legal IT Survey 1994, less than a quarter of firms use their database to monitor the success of initiatives, with 78% using them primarily (or exclusively) for mailing purposes

They shift control away from me – the expert

This point deals with a common objection from partners. They fear losing control of 'their' clients. They demand that all contact from the firm be channelled through them. The irony is that databases are more effective at this task than any single partner.

Such jealous protection of the client or contact is understandable. The relationship has been built on a personal basis. That partner is responsible for the client and needs to be sure that professional and personal standards are maintained.

Yet such a view is reductive. Seeking to protect the client relationship, can merely constrict it. As Kim Tasso observes, 'lawyers must learn to trust their colleagues with their clients'.

158

They are too complicated to work properly

Only if they are set up badly, under-resourced, or inappropriate to the task for which they were supposedly specified. It is essential to keep marketing records, for example, as simple as possible. While there may be great attractions in recording all the interests of a client or contact, that should be treated as a secondary stage, with core information (name, address, appellation etc) being supplemented only by a simple, wide 'Type of Business' categorisation and a coding of his or her legal interests.

When building a database, complexity is the enemy. When you have mastered the basics, by all means consider the value-added elements. But not before. Kim Tasso again: 'It is better by far to set one or two key objectives for the system and succeed with them than to aim for a really complex system that achieves nothing.'

Using a database properly should overcome most objections. The client partner can be informed of all mailings as part of the database management. Since several partners may work with a client, the database proves a more efficient way of monitoring and updating accurate client details than individual partner policing and occasional memoranda.

Opportunities for cross-selling of expertise within the firm are much more likely to arise from database records than from inspiration from that client partner, or from notes around the partnership, requesting 'any contacts you can think of, to whom this event might appeal'.

How to choose a database

To get this right, you need to do some work in advance. A working group should be gathered, comprising representatives from management, IT and marketing. Whoever runs your mailing lists should be present.

The following questions need to be answered, and those answers agreed on, before inviting suppliers to pitch for your business:
- What tasks do we need the database to perform?
- What do we want the system to achieve?
- What are the benefits we want to gain?
- Do we want a simple system, or a sophisticated one?
- Which fields do we want (ie on which criteria will we want to glean information, or select clients and contacts for future mailings)?

- Is the database going to have to integrate into the existing computing system?
- Who is going to be responsible for operating the database?

There is always a risk that the database becomes a hot potato. Make sure that there is consensus achieved at the meeting about who will control the system, who will manage it, and who will have access.

Ensure that one person writes a brief following this meeting. This should include a specification of what is wanted back? People who work in the IT field tend to talk gobbledygook. They get hung up on the features of their systems, and rarely know how to communicate benefits to the client. Therefore it is worth putting together a brief that makes it absolutely clear that your IT representative can be primed separately with the exciting stuff about megabytes, parallel processing and so on, but that you expect the presentation to you to have one key objective: to demonstrate how the database meets your specified goals.

Give the supplier a hypothetical situation – the most complex one you can create, based on your likely objectives. Instruct the database representatives to explain to you, in terms that you can understand, in pictorial form and in practical demonstrations, exactly how their proposed system would allow you to proceed effectively.

There are a lot of people trying to sell you databases, configured specifically to the legal, accountancy or your own particular professional marketplace. It is a buyer's market. Demand to see what you want to see. Don't be fobbed off with technospeak or theory. Don't commit any money to a project until systems have completed trial periods successfully.

Finally, ensure that one person has overall control of the system and is given the time and inputting resources to ensure than data is entered, updated and checked regularly. No one should be enabled to amend information without this person's knowledge and authorisation. If all secretaries have access, make sure they have no means to add or delete. Only then will centralised information be controllable and have any chance of remaining accurate.

Summary

- Plan exactly what you want to achieve, in terms of benefits to your Firm. Compile a list of options to choose from, rather than brainstorm through abstractions.
- Talk to your contacts in other firms. Ask to see their database systems. Find out what works and what does not. Find out what the teething problems were.
- Spend time putting together a plain English brief to potential suppliers. This should specify the tasks a database is expected to achieve and the degree of simplicity/complexity you desire.
- If you meet a sales person who can communicate in your language – not the language of a computer – put their company at the head of your list.
- Make sure you see a demonstration of the tasks you want to achieve. Do not be fobbed off with something 'similar'. It will be different.
- Whatever the extent of its functional complexity, buy a system that is easy to use. Do not use something that talks to you in codes which take weeks to master, and where a failure to type in a meaningless formula leaves you combing the manuals for hours.
- Always go for the straightforward and user-friendly option. Avoid the bangs and whistles version.
- Make sure you establish guarantees for appropriate training and after-sales support. There will be problems, even with the best systems. A decent hotline and a local trouble-shooter can make the difference between a revolution in office efficiency – and a revolution in the office.
- Ensure that your existing IT records are converted into the new system, and that you don't need to recreate the wheel. Ask to have your mailing lists converted into database form.
- Pilot the system. Commit to purchase only when it is absolutely clear that your preferred choice can achieve all the aims set out in the brief. This certainty only flows from a convincing demonstration.
- It is vital to believe in what you are buying. Only total confidence in the system will lead you to allocate enough time and staff resources to database operating and training. Asking a secretary or two to add database maintenance and operation to their list of occasional tasks is the best way to ensure immediate redundancy of the system.

- Educate your partners and staff. Set up demonstrations of what the system can and cannot achieve.
- Make certain that raw information flows to the database operator. Use and keep hard copy pro formas as a back-up record.
- Establish a simple, easy way to extract and relay information within the firm. Without regularly updated data, the system will become flawed very quickly.
- Learn to crawl. Then walk before you run. Do not expect your investment to pay off in a matter of weeks. Iron out problems through trial runs, on simple tasks. Leave the clever stuff for later.
- Use and enthuse. Only by communicating with partners and staff how the database has made a difference will you create a database culture, where visible benefits of use outweigh natural conservatism. You will face initial suspicion: counter it, don't let it grow.

11 Exhibitions

What is the point of exhibiting?

Manning a stand at an exhibition has two purposes. The least important is to convey or receive information, by means of corporate literature, collecting business cards, etc. The real *raison d'être* is to meet people. If you do not want to invite people onto your stand, are not sure why you are there and would really rather be in the office getting fee-earning work done – then stay in the office.

Some would argue that if you have a major role to play in a market you must be seen at that market's premier conference and exhibition. However, the wrong approach can be counter-productive, or even destructive, through (for example) an inappropriate display or unmanned stand.

It is never enough to simply turn up. There is no point in exhibiting unless a firm is committed to doing the job properly. A half-hearted exhibitor is a liability, and an expensive one at that. The cost of a stand and stand space is considerable, and is allied to the time spent on non-billable work plus the administrative tasks necessary to put an appropriate representation of the firm into place.

Lynn Hill of Taylor Johnson Garrett warns against devoting all this effort to the wrong occasion. 'Most exhibitions are a waste of time. Only consider going to one that is closely targeted to the audience you want to meet.'

Despite the investment in time and money, a (well targeted) exhibition can be one of the most effective means of promoting a law firm. Stand visitors appreciate the chance to chat informally about issues that concern them. As long as you are at the right place, you should meet people working in areas where you have relevant expertise.

The fact that you have made the effort to exhibit demonstrates your commitment to that market sector. An exhibition gives visitors the opportunity to select literature, perhaps adding to their knowledge of the specific services you offer and your areas of expertise. Thus an exhibition stand can convey your strengths forcibly to the right people.

EXHIBITIONS

How to choose the right exhibition

Let us assume that a firm, strong in a particular sector, decides to exhibit. How does it choose an appropriate venue?

Several means suggest themselves. Often the best exhibitions run alongside conferences. Associations and groups within the sector may run those conferences, or may be able to refer you to the appropriate organiser.

Clients, invited as delegates, should be able to advise on their favoured conferences and exhibitions. Various commercial organisations publish lists of forthcoming exhibitions, on a regional, national and international basis.

The trade press will cover annual conferences and exhibitions in their sector, often devoting whole features or even issues to the major events. A quick word with an editor can save weeks of research. However, be aware that if the magazine is the organ of a particular organisation, the editor is unlikely to miss the opportunity to plug that organisation's annual gathering of the clans.

Once you have compiled your list of possible venues, you need to establish the following:

- Direct cost of exhibiting (stand space, stand building, hotels and travel).
- The delegate profile (are they chief executives and finance directors? Is the visitor likely to be a decision maker in providing legal work?).
- Whether the timing is a problem (does the exhibition clash with another event or the firm's year end, for example? Does it interfere with the holiday plans of key partners?).

Most of this information can be found simply by calling the exhibition organisers and asking for the previous year's exhibitor and delegate lists – plus information on current plans. Bear in mind that the best way of researching a venue is to attend one year, with a view to booking space at the next year's event while you are *in situ*.

If your decision making process allows you to do this, it may enable you to get a good site for your stand – or at least head the list of applicants. At a popular exhibition, most exhibitors will re-book their existing or preferred spot, putting newcomers at an obvious disadvantage.

164

Location

Great debates are often held over the right and wrong place for a stand to be sited. There are those who swear by being at the main entrances or exits, while others demand central locations. Some cling to side walls, believing that their visitors enjoy window shopping on the periphery. Studies have been done to investigate through traffic, trends, habits and preferences. The upshot?

Common sense remains the best judge of location. You need to be in a main aisle. Quite simply, you need to be somewhere where you can be seen. Whether you are in the middle, on the end, in the centre or on the edge makes very little difference. It is better to be on the floor of entry to an exhibition, and in the main hall, but being up or at the end of a flight of stairs is rarely cause for concern.

It is, of course, a problem if you are hidden away in a satellite location. To avoid such a fate, look at the previous year's exhibitor locations – or preliminary bookings for the current year. Ring up a few of the companies or firms represented and ask them about their experience of previous years. That will give you an idea of contemporary wisdom with regard to best sitings and visitor behaviour.

The best option, once again, is to visit the year before and spend time watching the eddying visitors. Where do they congregate? Where are the areas of peak traffic?

Don't ask the exhibition organisers, since invariably they will tell you that all is rosy in the garden and that the few locations left are in prime niche locations.

If you think you are being fobbed off with a poor location, but still want to take one of the few remaining stands, haggle with the exhibition organisers. Point out the pillar blocking line of sight, or your being hidden in a corner away from the main walkways. Unless the last stand locations are bound to be sold, you should be able to negotiate a discount on the space. Most exhibition organisers, for obvious reasons, are paranoid about being left with unsold space, and will happily accept a reduction in costs towards the end of their drive to fill halls.

If, despite all this, you find yourself landed with a poor location, you will simply have to work harder. This will entail spending more time away from the stand, meeting visitors or delegates and walking the floor. The author, however, stops short of endorsing the advice given by one 'expert'. Hiring a popcorn making machine 'to attract visitors onto the stand by smell' somehow does not feel quite right for a law firm.

Shell scheme – or space only?

You will need to decide whether to book a shell scheme or take your own bespoke stand. A shell scheme is usually a basic structure, on the walls of which you can add shelves, display units or signage. It will incorporate a fascia with your name on it, carpeting and lighting.

Exhibition organisers discount space-only bookings, but the 10% or so saved is more than offset by significant extra costs in providing your own stand. The obvious advantage is that you should gain a more impressive display, customised to your particular needs.

Bespoke stands

There are a hundred and one different styles and approaches to stand building. Each stand has to serve a specific purpose and reflect a unique identity. Obviously, therefore, there is no such thing as a template stand. However, a little forward thinking before commissioning a stand can ensure that the most efficient and effective design is created.

It is important that your design is modular. There is little or no chance of your being able to book the same dimensions at more than one or two venues, so an inflexible design will cost a fortune in adaptations. Even if you were to find identical space at more than one venue, you may find that you need to account for an obtruding pillar or want to allocate more room on the stand to entertaining or displays. The more adaptability built into the design, the fewer problems will arise when it comes to modifying to perform a specific function.

If your corporate identity is strong and fixed, make sure that it is prominent in the design. If it is not, ensure that it is less integral – ie it can be updated without a complete stand rebuild.

Allow for storage. If you have five people on a stand on a rainy day, there needs to be room for umbrellas, raincoats and briefcases. Additionally, you will need room out of sight for a waste bin and extra documents/display material. Building storage into display areas, seating or other parts of the stand structure should be considered.

If you know you are going to attend several exhibitions, plan the signage for all of them at once. Ideally, frame wording that relays a central corporate message, common to all events, in addition to tailored signs or displays for each one. This saves on both cost and time.

Ensure that you have sufficient display receptacles, space and access for your future needs, or conversely that you have sufficient literature or display material to fill display areas.

You may want to incorporate a safe, so that a mobile phone and other valuables can be taken to an exhibition and left safely on the stand. Additionally, depending on space, a fridge can be a great boon over a period of time, perhaps for storing wine used in visitor hospitality.

Promotional literature

Every stand has some form of corporate literature on it. Most law firms will display their main brochure and information pertinent to the exhibition. It is important to achieve a balance between hype – the services we offer you – and information – here's some free text relevant to the problems you are likely to encounter in your field.

However, unlike the standard professional document where content is important and form considered relatively unimportant, here the opposite is true. The way the literature looks and is displayed is more important than its content, particularly if the latter is promotional rather than factual. In a hall full of people vying for visitors' attention, your literature display must look enticing.

Differentiate yourself

What does a law firm have to offer? People and literature. Neither is likely to make your display stand out from all the others in the hall.

A little imagination needs to go into planning the stand. What can be added, to attract attention? Obvious showmanship will not sit easily with your natural style, but running a competition may work. This will not only give you a natural opening for conversations, but will also appeal to visitors' natural interest in getting something for nothing.

Make the competition simple – two or three multiple choice questions, a magnetic dartboard – anything that lightens the tone without being too facile.

Alternatively, put something visually compelling on your stand. Commission a work of sculpture or art relevant to the theme of the exhibition, or to the firm, and display it prominently. For a particularly important event, it may be worth shooting a brief video and showing this on a rolling tape. If this is done, make sure it is done with impact – hire a large-screen television.

Make sure you support your presence at an exhibition by letting your clients know you are there. Send them complimentary tickets and an invitation to join you for a glass of wine. The exhibition organisers will fall over themselves to help, since you will be targeting their audience for them.

Consider advertising in the trade press, well in advance of the exhibition, particularly if you plan to unveil any new service at the event, or if one of your partners is speaking on a topical subject at the associated conference.

Preparing for an exhibition

Depending on the circumstances, you may need to start preparing your firm's attendance anything up to 18 months in advance. With an annual exhibition, that means six months prior to the previous event. Alternatively, you can get away with a few weeks' preparation, although this is hard on the nerves of all concerned.

Most organisers will make life easy for you by sending a succession of pro formas to be completed. Nevertheless, there are exceptions and it is easy to miss a deadline. The checklist at the end of this chapter may prove useful in ensuring that the stand on the day looks like the stand you planned.

Exhibition techniques

Once on the stand, it is extremely easy to let natural reticence take over. The British are particularly bad at exhibitions. Leading the pack is the professional practice. As a group, the professions often display an in-built reluctance to exhibit themselves. Lawyers, accountants, surveyors, architects – all shrink back amidst their wares, or convey strong 'go away' messages through body language.

Because it is not a skill that comes naturally, lawyers need to learn how to exhibit. Therefore, the following guidelines may come in useful.

First of all, stand up. Don't ever sit down on the job. Look alert and friendly.

168

Your task is to engage people in conversation. This is naturally much easier if you know the person. Hail them from within your stand, so that they have to come in. Ask them how they are progressing with a particular piece of work. Allude to your/the firm's current activities in this area. Draw out as much information as you can (and make sure that when you return to the office, this is relayed to all appropriate fee earners).

For anyone unknown to you, the procedure is less simple. Invite them to take part in your on-stand competition, or to take away your literature. Better still, ask them a question. An open question.

An example of a closed question is 'would you like a copy of our brochure?'. The likely result is a 'No thank you', and a swift exit. Even an affirmative falls short of establishing a conversation.

An open question begins with a who, what, where, when, why or how. It demands a response. It drags the individual into conversation.

If all this sounds coercive, then the author has got the tone about right. Much as we'd like clients and contacts to descend on our stands with whoops of delight, it happens but rarely. The passing delegate wants to window-shop, but isn't sure what he or she is looking for. It is up to you to draw this individual out.

That is how exhibitions pay for themselves.

The process may go something like this:

- 'Hello. What do you know about Fudge & Morris?'
- 'Not very much. Aren't you big in intellectual property?'
- 'That's right. But recently we've developed a specialisation in providing commercial property for inward investors. That's why we're here. What aspect are you involved in?'
- 'I work in corporate finance. Do you have any kind of track record?'
- We most certainly do. In fact, three of our partners ...'

Two minutes later you have a business card, a clear idea of a problem your potential client needs to overcome, and a duty to follow up via the appropriate partner.

An alternative approach, and one better suited to the softer-selling solicitor, is not to communicate one's selling message, but to draw out the visitor's needs.

- 'Hello. I see you're looking at our intellectual property brochure. What work do you do in that area?'
- 'Um, none really. I was just browsing.'
- 'So you're not involved in any intellectual property work at the moment?'

- 'No.'
- 'What sort of legal services do you think might be of use to you in the near future?'
- 'Probably minor litigation and some funding advice.'
- 'In that case, let me give you these information sheets and my card. I'll write on it the names of our partners who specialise in those areas. May I ask them to contact you?'

Yes, of course some people will find adopting even this gentle persuasion too aggressive. They will argue that visitors to the stand will be put off by any form of explicit promotion of the firm. Unfortunately, such a view cannot be allowed to prevail. If it does, do not exhibit.

In either of the above hypothetical cases, your new contact will have developed a positive impression of your firm, new-found knowledge of your expertise, and a point of contact. The brochures or information that he or she takes away are incidental in themselves, but provide background and back-up for the messages taken from your stand.

A word of warning for the enthusiastic. It is poor form to leap from your stand onto the back of a hapless passer-by. It is marginally preferable to stand with a frozen grin at the front of your stand. Much better is the relaxed, dignified yet friendly and accessible approach outlined above.

Feel free to browse through your own literature, adopting a suitably rapt expression. This allows you to keep an eye on your surroundings, without looking over-eager (or bored). Reading the paper or a book is not on. Leaving the stand unattended is usually adjudged equally sinful. The exception would be when the exhibition runs alongside a conference, and all delegates are attending a session.

If there are several of you on the stand at any one time, and a hush falls over proceedings, this should be seen as an opportunity to walk the floor. Look into how your competitors are faring and read their documents. Visit the stands of any potential clients. Strike up conversations with anyone who can give you their impression of the exhibition. This can help endorse your recommendations as to whether the stand should be re-booked for next time around.

Record keeping

Don't be satisfied with a system that leaves all new contact information in the head of the person who happened to be on the stand when a delegate visited. Exhibition attendance should be part of a concerted effort to build on and expand the firm's contacts – not those of selected individuals.

Thus, all who man stands should complete pro formas to note pertinent information about visitors. These documents should be collected together and all information logged centrally – ideally onto a database recording system.

Such pro formas should enable you to note whether an immediate and specific follow up is required and who should make it.

Follow up

So you have got through two or three days on stand. You have re-booked for next year. A few old faces have been greeted, and some new ones memorised. A handful of business cards has been added to your collection. You may even have remembered to fill in your client-recording pro forma. What now?

The tendency is to relax, think you've done your duty and go back to the real world. This wastes an opportunity. Whoever looks after the firm's database needs to receive a report on who was met. This could be via a pro forma or a phone call, but it needs to relay what they were interested in and their basic address details. 'Meeting someone at an exhibition', says Jennie Gubbins, 'is merely a step along the way. Failing to follow up an encounter risks letting a good potential contact go cold'.

Partners and colleagues need to be notified of the interests mentioned by contacts. If someone is planning to expand their premises or operations, perhaps a property or funding specialist needs to add them to a seminar mailing list? Observations made by people met on a stand can often form the perfect excuse for a follow-up letter. This might enclose information, or merely reiterate your firm's interest in working with the contact on business discussed, if appropriate.

It is a good idea to grade contacts on the record sheets. All those receiving an A grade should receive personalised, tailored letters immediately after the event. B grades should follow as soon as possible, with other grades perhaps receiving a stock letter.

All those who took stints on the stand should be encouraged to report on the way the exhibition worked or failed. A brief questionnaire should be circulated. Alternatively, and preferably, a short meeting should be held to determine what should be done differently next

171

time around. This should be held immediately, while ideas are fresh. A meeting held two months before next year's exhibition will be of limited use.

Checklist of administrative stand arrangements

- Decide on whether you want to book space only or a shell scheme.
- Book stand.
- If space only, find, brief and commission a stand builder. If a shell scheme, plan what you are going to use/buy to fill the space.
- Plan what publications you want to display. Commission these internally if they do not already exist. Give an artificially early deadline.
- Plan how many people should be on the stand during all shifts. An idea of the programme can be gauged from the previous year.
- Establish whether you will be holding or attending dinners or evening receptions. This will affect both accommodation and stand staffing arrangements.
- Book restaurants as needed.
- Book hotel accommodation.
- If the exhibition runs alongside a conference, investigate speaker opportunities through the organisers. Book attendees in as delegates, as required.
- Assign attendees to stand duty.
- Arrange bagging for all attendees (usually via the event organisers).
- Establish when the stand can be built and dismantled. Inform stand designer.
- Book telephone, stand photography and catering, as required (usually using the exhibition organisers' pro formas).
- Put together press packs (press release and supporting photography or background material) if you have anything to announce at the event. Arrange for these to be displayed at the press desk or office.
- Plan on-stand attractions, such as competition, displays or giveaways.
- Arrange advertising as necessary in the event handbook.
- Ensure that any free editorial to which you are entitled is supplied to trade magazines or in the conference handbook: details will be sent to you by the event organisers.
- Brief members of the firm on what to do when on the stand.
- Compile all information germane to those who are attending the exhibition. Include copies of stand manning rota, useful telephone numbers, maps, travel details, local taxi firms, location of hotels and restaurants, conference organiser details and notes on how the stand should be run/left at the end of each session. Circulate this document the week before the event.

Summary

- Visit an exhibition the year before you exhibit. Talk to exhibitors about their experiences.
- Take away copies of visitor/delegate and exhibitor lists/numbers.
- Provisionally book space as early as possible – preferably at the previous year's exhibition.
- Assess which locations are the best (delegate flow can be affected by such factors as neighbouring stands or proximity to a main entrance, refreshments or the conference hall).
- If you are booking space only (ie not a shell scheme), choose a location which fits the existing dimensions of your stand.
- Talk to the exhibition organisers. Ask their advice about stand fitting, favoured locations, promotional opportunities etc. Find out which stands are unlikely to be made available through the incumbent re-booking.
- Find out from the organisers how long you will have before making a final decision on stand location – ie when you have to confirm your provisional booking. Ask for their estimation of the date by which all stands are likely to be booked.
- Design your stand and its display well in advance. Agree signage working and key messages internally.
- Encourage those who will man the stand to book themselves away from the office as if it were a client meeting. Try to create an understanding that attendance is an obligation, not an option to be discarded lightly because of other work commitments.
- Hold a meeting or workshop to inculcate exhibition skills into those who will be attending.
- Produce something unusual, visually attractive or compelling to differentiate the stand.
- Delegate attendees to attend all possible events and entertain visiting clients.
- Encourage feedback re advisability of re-attending next event – and opportunities to improve performance.
- Investigate opportunities to address any conference alongside which the exhibition is running.
- Produce publicity material germane to the delegate profile (having acquired a list of previous delegates).
- Consider whether a press pack should be produced for display on the press desk at the exhibition.
- Keep an eye on all administrative arrangements, finalising all preparations at the earliest opportunity.

Hints and tips

- Book hotel accommodation at the earliest opportunity – ideally in or near the exhibition venue. Many hotels are booked a year or even years in advance of regular events.
- Find stand builders through the exhibition organisers, a colleague's recommendation, or through advertisements in a conference and exhibition publication (see a media directory). The best way is to visit an exhibition and ask for the name of the people who designed your favoured stand.
- Keep contact recording sheets on the stand. These should be single sheets of paper on which encounters can be noted and to which business cards should be attached. Each should note the name of the individual and his or her contact details, areas of interest and the nature of any proposed follow up, as well as the person best placed to conduct follow up activity.

12 Seminars

Almost all publicity activities have their detractors. Some lump all advertising together as crass; exhibitions are expensive; brochures are never read; media relations is an ego trip. These views contain enough small elements of truth to leaven their wrong-headedness.

The objection to seminars is that they're so difficult to set up, in terms of time and effort. If you want easy options, look elsewhere. That said, recalcitrant lawyers tend to offer far less resistance to seminars than to other forms of marketing support.

The reason lies in the direct nature of the seminar. You invite people to come to your event and meet them in the flesh. A seminar provides pertinent information to people who are only there because they are interested. In marketing terms, they are hot prospects.

At an exhibition, it is often chance that drives the right person to the right stand to talk about a subject on which both can do business.

No one hands over a brochure and expects to discuss its contents with the recipient. Even a carefully targeted letter suffers from the sender's inability to react immediately to a (potential) client's response.

Whereas a seminar brings lawyer and potential new business into proximity. It raises explicitly a subject of mutual interest, generating grounds for further exploratory discussion. It serves as a forum in which to display expertise.

Trowers & Hamlins' David Mosey puts this into perspective. 'The best means of practice development,' he observes, 'is a demonstration of your skills. Failing that, nothing beats a captive audience, heavily chaperoned by your colleagues, watching you in action at a seminar.'

If delegates are charged only to cover costs, or indeed if the seminar is given gratis, it serves to establish goodwill. A seminar is an occasion on which legal advice can come without a bill.

The chance of picking up work directly from a seminar is higher than through any other promotional activity, with the possible exception of highly targeted corporate hospitality. Though no marketing event can ever guarantee that work will arise purely from the event itself, seminars provide the most fertile ground for converting awareness of expertise into instructions. Indeed, Lynn Hill believes that 'every seminar has given us new work'.

When to hold a seminar

Topicality is as much of a lure as information. It is important to hold a seminar as soon as possible after a development arises that will lead contacts to seek explanations and viewpoints. This means that forward planning is essential.

Do not put on a seminar unless you are sure it meets a need. If possible research that need. Call people who might be invited, to gauge interest.

If legislative change in an area likely to affect a sizeable cross-section of your clients is expected in July, start planning as early as possible. Ideally you will want to put on the seminar immediately, though a delayed date may be sensible should the legislation not go to timetable. However, since conference organisers, competitors and other professionals will be alive to the same opportunity you have spotted, and will be publicising their own events, you need to set a date and issue invitations at least two months in advance.

Avoid holding events on Mondays and Fridays. On the former, people will have yet to get their feet back under the table; on the latter, last minute work will take precedence before the onset of the weekend. Treat the whole of August as a Monday! Everyone is either on holiday, wishing they were on holiday, or overwhelmed by the delegated work of colleagues who have gone on holiday.

If you are aiming for a particularly defined target market, check that your preferred date does not clash with an industry event. If you want to attract fund managers, there is little point in selecting the date of their Institute's annual jamboree, or the AGM of a large and important PLC. As always, ring around a sample for advice and to check diaries.

Planning

Once you have established the need for a seminar, start by naming it. This may sound trite, but it is an essential first step. It will clarify what it is you wish to cover and will give a universal reference point for all those involved. If the firm is involved in several speaker opportunities, a working title is essential to avoid confusion.

Try to come up with a title that attracts attention. Entice delegates with the prospect of solutions to problems. A title such as

MAKE THE MOST OF YOUR LAWYER

is far less interesting than

USING THE LAW TO SAVE PROBLEMS, TIME AND MONEY

Which is more likely to attract you to a seminar?

DIRECTORS DUTIES AFTER CADBURY

or

HOW TO AVOID LIABILITY
(Ten Practical Steps for Directors)

With preparation of transcripts, visual material, delegate information and even the core text often left to the last minute, it is tempting for marketeers to lose all patience and perspective. Wilde Sapte's Matthew Fuller counsels, adopting an educational rather than confrontational approach. 'It's important to work with busy fee earners, acknowledging time pressures, but conveying the dangers. Last minute preparation invariably leads to irrecoverable errors. Only if this is accepted do you have a chance of enforcing timetables.'

Finally, ensure that the seminar is worth holding. Check that it offers scope and relevance, in the right ambience, at an acceptable cost (see Fig 20 on p 180).

Partner involvement

It is vital to have one person, at a senior level, take 'ownership' of a seminar. The pressures of day to day work will always encroach on a speaking engagement. Unless someone is charged with whipping recalcitrant participants into action, administration, drafting, rehearsals and mailing arrangements will fall by the wayside.

Who should speak?

As a general rule, no one should be on a platform for more than 40 minutes. If you have two hours of information to impart, make sure there are at least three speakers, to ring the changes. Your greatest

Fig 20

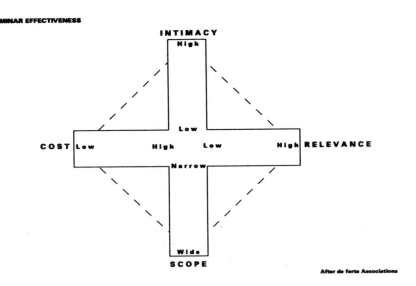

experts may be your worst speakers and vice versa. Choose the right horse for the course.

If your junior staff are better presenters and better informed than the partners on a particular subject, put them behind the lectern – not the household name who may stumble over detail. Make sure you arrange presentation training first and set up at least one full dress rehearsal. The chairman can make capital out of the non-speaking expert's reputation, by alluding to his or her being available at post-seminar drinks.

Consider inviting a guest speaker, to broaden the range of the seminar and lend an air of objectivity to what might otherwise be seen as purely a marketing exercise (which of course it is).

Who should be invited?

Everyone who could possibly be interested in the subject. Think laterally. If the subject is industry-specific, obviously there is no point in widening the net to beyond that industry, but if the subject is generic, then a seminar invitation provides the perfect opportunity to renew old contacts, introduce yourself to new prospects, and market across your firm's clients.

Obviously, if the firm has a working database, this is the first port of call. Draw up a bespoke seminar invitation list. If time allows (and it should), check that the list is current by circulating it internally. Ask for new names and details, and for any personalised messages to be added from within the firm. Ensure that all updates are relayed to the database.

If no database exists, or if it does not include organisations or individuals working in the areas you cover, trawl your firm for contacts before looking outside. Send round details of the seminar, who it will appeal to, and a request for extra invitees. Unfortunately, there are still those who guard jealously their own contacts, at the expense of the firm as a whole. Less inexcusably, busy colleagues may not be prepared to spend time seeking out addresses for their own contacts. Allow for this. They may be more amenable to scribbling a list of names and organisations. You or your secretary can then research each individual's address and title.

If you are targeting a specific market, you may be able to set up the seminar as a joint venture with someone prominent in the field, or with a professional body active in that area. As well as providing a speaker, kudos and possibly financial support, this body may well have mailing lists invaluable to the success of your event.

Once again, planning in advance allows you to capture seminar partners; wait too long, and they will stage their own event or be invited to participate in others.

In some cases, you may need to attack a 'cold' marketplace, where you know few contacts. In this case, lists of contacts can be bought from List Brokers. Contact colleagues or check directories/advertisements to find out who specialises in compiling information in your required sector. Bear in mind that responses to a cold mailing may be as low as 1% of all people mailed. This provides another reason why mailing well in advance of the event can be helpful: it allows a secondary mailing if the first elicits a low response.

Choice of venue

There are literally thousands of places in the UK with facilities for seminars, ranging from plush hotels to eccentric locations boasting novelty, as opposed to familiarity. Calm efficiency is the differentiator that matters. Seminars can be worrisome affairs; the last thing you can accept is being left to a DIY approach, or being left with someone who is unable to put problems right when they occur.

Select a location near to you, if you can. This will help in terms of regular visits, rehearsals, or any emergency needs for documentation to be relayed from the firm.

If you find a venue staffed by competent people, don't be tempted to change until you are sure that your regular delegates are sick of the sight of the place. The chances are that this will never happen, since they will appreciate knowing their way around as much as you do.

While the cost of room hire is obviously an important consideration, so too are accessibility by road and rail, room decor, technical facilities, proximity to your offices, parking availability, cost of refreshments, additional costs of ancillary rooms for any entertainment purposes, cloakroom facilities, flexibility over your specific needs and the host of 'minor' things that make or break a seminar. Always ask for hidden costs to be made explicit. Different venues have different policies when it comes to charging for rehearsal time, use of microphones and audio visual equipment, cancellation costs and so forth.

For example: what happens when an overhead projector's lightbulb blows during a presentation? Is there someone to fix it? If the signage announcing the room in which your seminar is to be held spells your name wrong, how easy is it to put matters right? If the chairman of a seminar preceding yours decides unilaterally to extend his event into your allocated slot, how do the staff solve the problem?

When you meet in advance to rehearse the seminar, raise these questions. Do not proceed until you receive satisfactory responses. If the venue performs as well as can reasonably be expected, they should be rewarded by your continued custom. Efficiency here reflects well on you. Chaos is deemed your problem by delegates, not that of the venue staff.

When booking a venue, you are bound to be asked, 'How many people are going to attend your event?' Whether you are mailing 100 or 10,000, you can never be sure how many will respond, who will register, and who will turn up on the day.

Therefore, any organisation that is willing to hold alternative rooms for you until you can confirm numbers is to be guarded jealously. Booking a room for 60, and then having only 20 delegates is embarrassing. Having a fall back option, and being able to transfer to this smaller room, means no delegate ever knows that the response was not as anticipated.

If you have a glut of acceptances, you may need to write to an over-flow of delegates, asking if they would mind re-booking for another day. However, this is still a poor solution, best avoided by provision-ally booking a larger room.

Such a conundrum provides a strong argument for inviting delegates well in advance, to keep your options open.

If you are providing a seminar on a topical issue, inform the media. Many trade and national publications have sections promoting forth-coming events that may appeal to readers. A press release outlining details can be a most effective means to free publicity.

Keep your colleagues informed of progress, through notes, depart-mental reports, items in the internal newsletter, or in person. If you can generate excitement within your firm, this should translate to an easi-er task in persuading your peers to attend the seminar and meet the guests. Motivated colleagues will motivate delegates; reluctant atten-dees, goaded by a three line whip, may simply cause damage.

Timetable and administration

Whoever is responsible for the marketing and administration of the seminar should sit down with the individual allocated overall respon-sibility for the event as soon as a date has been agreed (and checked for potential clashes with internal/external events). A timetable, out-lining duties and those responsible for their performance, should be drawn up.

Artificial deadlines should be ascribed to all activities, allowing lee-way in the event of illnesses, work pressures, bloody-mindedness, and the plethora of excuses that can always be relied on to interrupt a smooth run-in to a seminar. It should be impressed on all parties that these deadlines are set in stone and must not be transgressed.

Dates and individual responsibility should be allocated to the fol-lowing:

- Production of a written timetable, incorporating the elements below.
- Regular update meetings.
- Timing and nature of event and entertainment/food/drinks.
- Provisional booking of venue.
- Agreement from speakers and chairman to participate.
- Finalisation of the programme.
- Briefing of speakers on preparation of material.

- Registration mechanism for delegates.
- Compilation of the mailing list.
- Drafting of invitation.
- Drafting of registration confirmation, including venue details, maps, tickets and badging as required.
- Internal notification of the event.
- Authorisation of mailing to all on list.
- Completion of presentations.
- Confirmation of venue booking.
- Manufacture of slides, overheads, other visual material.
- Mailing of invitation and response document/pro forma/envelope.
- Regular circulation of delegate list/numbers to speakers/organisers.
- Presentation rehearsals.
- Visit to venue, to check arrangements.
- Notification to venue of any special requirements.
- Preparation of badging.
- Preparation of delegate packs and transcripts.
- Preparation of visual display material (eg stand, brochures).
- Final arrangements for delivery of materials to venue.

In addition to the above, you will need to consider the work which can turn a seminar from a localised success or failure into something much larger – part of a sustained promotional effort. As Kim Tasso points out, 'to get the most from a seminar, you need a continuous programme of activities – mailshots, articles, conference attendance and lunches'.

Letter of invitation

Keep your mailing brief and to the point. Ideally, it should take the form of a single side of paper, with either an accompanying printed flier (giving additional details) or more simply, a pro forma reply slip. Consider adding a freepost envelope, or incorporating a post-paid card, for responses. Additionally or alternatively, you may want to set up a telephone booking service. If this is the case, make sure you have this permanently staffed, or diverted in cases of absence to an alternative telephonist.

Coordinator

One person should be in charge of administration, logging all bookings and informing the partnership of progress. It is vital that all communication concerning the event be channelled through this central point; the alternative is confusion over who is and who is not invited, attending or on the mailing list.

Follow up mailings

Those who register as delegates will need to be sent confirmation, along with any appropriate venue or route maps. Depending on the time built into the schedule, there may be an opportunity to mail a secondary invitation list, if response to the primary mailing has proved inferior to expectation.

Meetings

A well organised seminar programme will require very few meetings. However, these few are vital. Unless speakers and organisers gather together to chart progress against the agreed timetable (and that timetable becomes invaluable as deadlines begin to slip by), problems will occur. Keep the meetings happening, but keep them short.

Internal support

Strange though it may seem, many seminar organisers forget to communicate internally. Since the purpose of a seminar lies partly in a show of strength in a particular area of expertise, it is idiotic not to turn out in force, particularly to meet delegates after the speeches. Make sure that partners and fee earners are given the three line whip and that trainees or secretaries are also delegated to help with meeting, greeting and reception desk duties.

Badging

Don't produce delegate badges until the last possible moment. Make sure that you have blank badges at the event. Have a different style or colour for your own people, to differentiate them from delegates. Favour simple badges which can be affixed easily to the lapels of jackets. It is quite acceptable to have a sticky cloth badge rather than a twisted mass of clips and pins.

How many will turn up?

If you are charging for an event, most people will arrive on the day. However, if you are not charging, you can expect a proportion of your delegates to cancel at the last minute or simply not show. Assume a drop out rate of around 25% and you are unlikely to be far wrong.

Unless, of course, you have the bad luck to coincide with a disaster. One firm underwent the humiliation of taking a room for 200, expecting 100, yet speaking eventually to only 15 guests. To blame were a combination of a crisis in the delegates' particular market, freezing cold weather and a tube strike.

A huge amount depends on who you invite and how well they know you. See Fig 21 (opposite).

Preparation and presentation of material

One of the advantages of having a rehearsal ahead of the presentation date is that it focuses attention and increases the likelihood of planning. Too often, presentations are cobbled together the day before the event. Transcripts of botched presentations are handed out to complement garbled, unstructured talks.

It is important that delegates receive transcripts or full notes after the presentation, not before. On arrival, by all means hand out paper, pens, running order, biographies of speakers, delegate lists and so forth – but not anything that will distract the audience. Give them material to read, and they'll read it while the speakers are trying to gain their attention.

Extraordinary as it seems, there are those who not only read their presentations at seminars, but who insist on handing out verbatim transcripts. It is agonising to witness these people attempting to tell a joke which has just been read, word for word, by a bored yet incredulous audience.

So save the bulk of your notes until the end. Speakers should tell the delegates that notes will be made available, so that they do not scribble furiously during the presentation.

Notes and practical information are much more useful than transcripts. Usually, four pages boiled down to tables, charts, bullet points or brief facts outweigh 20 pages of straight transcript.

186

Fig 21

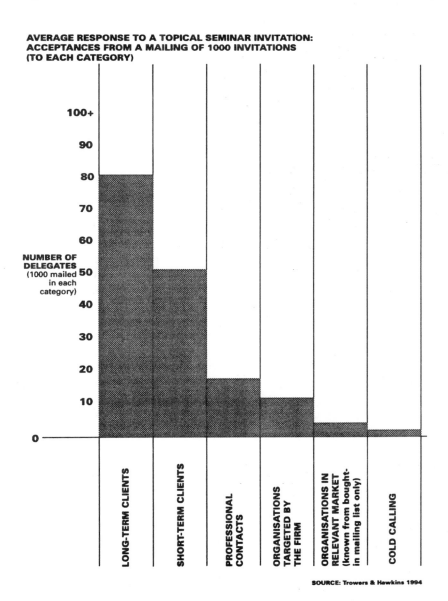

Preparing and giving presentations

- 'Giving speeches? You either can or you can't.'
- 'Learn how to communicate? I haven't time to waste on something I do every day of my life.'
- 'We offer a great service; it doesn't matter how we put ourselves across.'

Such views lead to poor client handling. Breakdowns in communication. And in the final analysis, a loss of business and income.

The skills required on a speaker platform are almost antithetical to those needed in producing a document, marshalling legal evidence, or in giving factual briefings.

Thus, good lawyers who are also good speakers tend to use complementary but different skills. Good lawyers who are bad speakers try to transpose what they already know and do well, to a forum where their efforts are likely to fall flat.

The specific skills appropriate to seminars and conferences are not restricted to these areas. Being able to present effectively improves performance in partner meetings, staff relations and in client meetings.

Everyone has sat through presentations where speakers have stumbled over their words and looked amateur in the process. However much ground was covered, they usually leave unclear the message they want to convey or the value of the service they are offering.

Some presenters are overwhelmed by the strength of the most senior speaker; others spend their entire presentation addressing and admiring their flashy slides.

So how do you go about preparing a presentation? A good idea is to read Chapter 6 of this book, on speaking in public! Alternatively, focus on the following key guidelines:

The blank sheet of paper is often where things start to go wrong. Many presenters decide that they will offload everything they know about a subject. Because the professions train in linear thinking, there is a tendency to write out a sequential series of unbroken facts.

The result is a stream of information, which overwhelms a dazed audience. A far better approach is to decide on a central message and theme the entire talk around it. Introduce the message at the beginning, refer to it throughout, and end with a reminder.

This backbone to your talk may seem repetitive to you, but only in this way will it become memorable to the audience.

As ideas are introduced, 'signpost' them. 'So, now that we've established X, where do we go from here? Let's look at Y.'

Being deadly dull is unforgivable. There are a hundred and one ways of being boring – and just as many of making yourself interesting. Try to use figurative, lively language. Use examples to explain how your subject affects the audience.

Which of the following is most likely to hold your attention:

- 'Taking legal advice in this area would be of great use to all companies, in averting the chance of inadvertent errors creeping into the *modus operandi* of each organisation. There is a risk that failing to prevent today leads to painful cures tomorrow.'

or

- 'What use is legal advice here? None at all – unless you want to guarantee your business health. Without the right advice – now – you could end up on the wrong side of both civil and criminal law.'

You'll notice that the second example sounds far more like everyday, idiomatic speech. For some reason, presenters in a formal situation often think they have to adopt language that is stilted, dry and dull. The more conversational you can be, the better you'll come across.

Don't allow yourself to slide into the conventional excuse that, as a lawyer, you are dealing with dry and dull information, therefore you can't bring it to life. Frankly, that's rubbish. There are no boring subjects, just boring speakers.

Another backsliding favourite is the view that your audience is too serious to accept a lightening of tone and a freshening of approach. Of course, there will always be the individual who prefers the turgid to the lively, but spare a thought for the majority who want to be captivated by your enthusiasm and vibrant delivery.

You want your firm to stand out from the crowd? Then you have to stand out, by giving presentations in the right way. Most don't.

Start with a flourish – perhaps with a hypothetical question, a powerful metaphor or a relevant anecdote -anything to arrest attention.

End with your central message – the idea you want everyone to leave the room remembering.

Practice is essential. Rehearse aloud on your own or with colleagues until you know your way around the presentation. Make absolutely sure that you have a rehearsal booked a week in advance of the event, and a dress rehearsal planned to precede the event itself.

Use cue cards for key words or headings. Make sure that before your seminar or conference you convene a full run-through. This will help you to pace yourself, iron out problems and gain confidence.

Once you have mastered your material you will be less concerned about drying up and will be able to give full attention to your performance.

Stand upright. Smile. Look as if you are enjoying yourself. Let your gaze include everyone.

Modulate your voice. Monotony kills a presentation. One useful technique is to start each sentence on a higher note, and end it on a lower one. Try this, building pauses between sentences. You'll find it lends authority and interest to what you say.

By all means use your hands, but in whole arm gestures, to underline what you are saying. Nervous hand flutterings and fiddles are merely distracting.

Avoid visual aids unless they add something to your presentation.

Finally, how do you conquer the great enemy, your nerves? You don't. Nerves are there to provide adrenaline. The goal is to control them, so that they work in your favour.

Adequate preparation and practice, allied to training in appropriate presentation techniques, means that your nerves will actually improve your performance.

It is a good idea to learn the first two or three sentences of your talk. Starting your speech is the most nerve-wracking time of all, so it is a good idea to go onto auto-pilot. Practice this introductory section until you can do it in your sleep. Getting off to a good start is vital, in creating initial impact with the audience, and in allowing you to calm yourself down.

Checklist: holding an event

General

- Produce a timetable integrating all of the following elements. This should count down to the event and indicate who takes responsibility for which actions.

Booking date and venue

- Agree potential dates with key players.
- Investigate venues.
- Check that the favoured venue has no simultaneous untoward (ie loud) events planned.
- Provisionally book the appropriate venue on an acceptable date.

- Visit and approve venue.
- Book in time for rehearsals (several days before if possible).
- Ensure booking allows time for setting up and clearing away.
- Confirm booking of venue.

Venue facilities

- Ascertain names of all venue contacts.
- Check the quality, nature and cost of food and drink.
- Determine ease of access and parking.
- Confirm that the room used can be blacked out (if needed) and is reasonably soundproofed.
- Investigate cleanliness and location of cloakroom and lavatories.
- Ensure adequate, visible event signage is arranged.
- Make sure that the room has sufficient flexibility to accommodate large or small numbers of guests (usually through room partitioning).
- Establish that there is easy access between rooms if more than one is used.
- Book any audio visual equipment needed.
- Check that the time of tea breaks and/or lunch breaks are agreed and that food and drink are confirmed.

Publicising

- Prepare invitation letter/invitation card copy.
- Compile mailing list.
- Consider supporting event through advertising and/or press release/photocall.
- Compile background material as needed (venue map, pro forma response sheet, etc).
- Print invitation card if appropriate.
- Conduct first mailing.
- Conduct any necessary telephone follow up.
- Check on any special dietary requirements, if appropriate.
- Send second letter confirming attendance details if appropriate.

Administrative preparation

- Keep a constantly updated list of attendees.
- Organise badging for attendees, speakers (and include spares).

SEMINARS

- Consider and arrange display material (stand, publications, signage, tent cards for speakers).
- Create (if not already extant) folders or wallets to hold papers.
- Put together pack for the day, including visitors book, scissors, blutak, pencils and pens, velcro, acrylic stands for display purposes, clock for speakers to time themselves.
- Produce slides or overheads.
- Draft ancillary information (speaker biographies, delegate list, service details).
- Produce folders/wallets of information, ready for event and post-event mailing to delegates/press.

Presentation preparation

- Prepare speech and handout notes.
- Draft text for slides or overheads.
- Hold rehearsals. Give speech, answer questions from the floor, gain familiarity with venue and technology.

On the day

- Arrive early.
- Set up (stand, slides, overhead projector, screen, seating plan).
- Ensure signage is in order.
- Check that duty manager is as anticipated.
- Conduct run through with speakers.

Day after

- Send packs to appropriate non-attendees.
- List what could be improved.
- Thank all those involved, including the venue.

192

Summary

- Hold a seminar when a subject is topical or when information meets an immediate and general need.
- Invite the right people: untargeted mailings are counterproductive.
- Hold events midweek if possible. Avoid August.
- The most enticing prospect is a short seminar, with detailed notes, held at the end of a day (though not too late), followed by a chance to meet speakers informally.
- Charging for seminars is not a good idea, unless the money is directed to a charitable cause. Only charge for a major conference, where the costs cannot be borne without subsidising contributions.
- Check that dates do not clash with any major draw on your target audience.
- Plan well in advance.
- Give the event an enticing title.
- Invitation copy should indicate that practical information will be forthcoming. Shape the seminar so that you are giving useful advice, not just legal theory.
- Ensure that there is sufficient enthusiasm and commitment from speakers to justify holding the event.
- Keep presentations short. Make sure speakers rehearse and know how to present (see Chapter 6).
- Compile invitation lists well in advance. Consider buying in lists or holding the event with an organisation that can supply an existing database of contacts.
- Select a venue that is nearby, if possible. When you find a place that works, stay there. If you get bored, don't move just for the change. Your guests will not be bored.
- Run through the event checklist (see p 183) with venue staff. Don't leave until you are happy with all responses.
- Where possible, hold as many rooms provisionally as you can, until likely numbers at the seminar become clear. Then confirm your requirements. Don't forget to make provisions for catering as well as presentations.
- Inform and invite the media, particularly if anything newsworthy is to be discussed at the seminar.
- Keep colleagues informed. Ask them to attend the seminar and any social events connected with the event.

Hints and tips

- Don't invite people to seminars through a Friday mailing. The invitation is likely to end up in the Monday pile. The Monday in-tray is invariably larger than that on any other day of the week.
- Hold back enough information so that the audience needs to instruct you, rather than head off alone. There is no point in giving free advice unless you get something back in return.

13 Research

Research is an offputting word. It conjures up images of laborious studies, or worse, of people interviewing us on the street. Yet without research, a law firm may be wasting a phenomenal amount of time, effort and potential profit.

If an organisation thinks that what the client wants is more important than anything else, it follows that it must know what the client wants.

Before it can know what the client wants, it needs to know who the client is, not just the person or persons with whom partners come into occasional contact, and also the structure, nature and ambitions of the organisation and its personnel.

Only then can a firm begin to offer appropriate services to its existing and potential clients.

The alternative to research

The only viable alternatives to researching client needs (doing nothing is discounted!) are to cut costs, thus making your offer potentially irresistible, or to differentiate yourself is such a way that clients cannot help but notice you.

Most law firms are bound to choose the research option. Configuring the nature of services offered to client needs is difficult, but it is compatible with a law firm's culture. Cutting costs is often seen as being at odds with quality service. It is also a high risk approach of dubious and unproven worth in a legal context. Differentiation is a fine concept, but achieving this in practice is next to impossible. To appear different means having to be dramatically different. This requires the sort of sea change that most firms find unthinkable. Differentiation can be achieved at product (service) level, but rarely throughout a law firm.

Therefore client oriented marketing driven by research becomes the only valid approach considered by the majority of law firms.

What you already know

A firm is a repository of information. Every individual has client and contact knowledge. Instructions and work in progress indicate what the immediate needs of clients, contacts and markets may be.

Meetings and telephone conversations constantly establish and update information. However, this information gathering is conducted on a piecemeal basis. Data is rarely gathered together, analysed and shared. Because of this, conclusions about what the client is or does are drawn individually and, at worst, arbitrarily.

Many research sources lie untapped within a law firm, simply because research has no place in the developmental strategy. For example, electronic and hard copy records abound, recording client details, work conducted, billing and payment information, profitability and bad debt histories.

Libraries are full of client information. On-line external and internal marketing databases, mailing lists and directories provide further examples of raw data.

Yet all this information is disparate. It can provide background (if gathered together) but it has no start point, common ground or established direction. In other words, it can be useful in specific circumstances, but it needs to be integrated into a framework in order to point convincingly to a proposed course of action.

Such information sources cannot give you the sort of detailed or sensitive information that you are likely to require when anticipating a significant course of action. If you need to know what your competitors are doing, what your clients will want next year, or what the market opportunities are in a specific sector, you will need to ask the outside world. And that means committing yourself to market research as part of practice development and the marketing of the firm.

What can be researched?

Obviously, anything lends itself to the questioning process. Less obviously, everything should. That questioning should be directed outwards (to the client) rather than inward ('what do we think about this?').

Research is not a rarefied marketing concept; it should be an integral step when considering any course of action. Any firm which becomes marketing driven (ie sets its strategy in response to the needs of the market) must, by definition, start with market research.

196

Fig 22   **INFORMATION-GATHERING AND
A FIRM'S EXISTING SOURCES OF KNOWLEDGE**

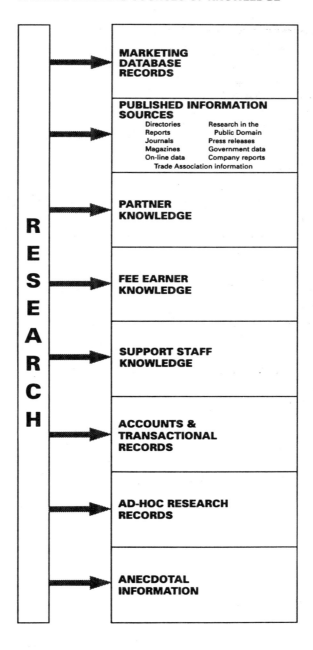

Research refers to the smallest steps ('ring a few favourite clients and find out what they think') as well as the largest ('let's appoint a consultancy to conduct a long-term programme to track client perception of our service').

Thus, it can be initiated on the back of almost any element of a firm's development, to meet almost any need. It may simply follow a decision to adapt the firm's logo or it may result from the possibility of opening a new office. Research may be used to investigate new market sectors or new service offerings. It can gauge client satisfaction or measure the likely response to a proposed merger of firms. It can indicate existing strengths and weaknesses, or determine recruitment objectives. Research can show what your competitors are doing and what the market is buying.

In all cases, it should drive, test or reevaluate the underlying beliefs in a firm's business and marketing plans.

The case for, and the case against

The case for research is the case for getting to know clients and their markets. The case against is comprised of the following:

- We are doing quite all right without wasting time establishing what we already know.
- The client thinks we know his business already; we'll look foolish if we are found asking questions.
- Research is too expensive, requiring too much in the way of staff time/consultancy fees.
- It's all about gut feeling, not research.

There is, or can be, some truth in most of these negative observations. If, for example, the first point is demonstrable, then research would be a luxury. Badly constructed research can be expensive, ineffective and counterproductive in terms of client response.

Yet, a firm can only truly say that it knows exactly what its clients want if the clients have been asked or researched. Any firm that values its clients and contacts must gather, monitor and share information about them. The evidence from several surveys points to a gulf between the views of clients and their lawyers in the UK, and to a need for better communication and tailoring of legal services.

When to research

Information should provide the foundation to any form of market penetration by a firm. Moving blindly in the dark is the alternative. Therefore, the only time research is not needed is when the required information is already known.

Even when facts are held by the firm, research can provide fresh insights, grounds for reinterpreting assumptions and additional information. Any progressive organisation needs to continually evaluate its commercial offerings, to ensure that what is provided satisfies the buyer, and its markets, to check that it represents long term prospects.

In conducting research, start from an assumption. As in writing a speech, a blank sheet of paper is of no help. If you start from a hypothesis, the research can test, temper or alter such a standpoint.

If you have a hypothesis, you should be able to anticipate possible findings. This will help you to plan alternative courses of action, dependent on the research results. Only by planning activity outlines well in advance will you be in a position to respond swiftly to the final results.

Such planning will help you to overcome the hurdles intrinsic to the conduct of a research exercise and the subsequent conversion into action. Information may need to be captured and held on a marketing database; it may require extensive use of consultants and high expenditure. Significant staff resources may need to be diverted to collate, assess and communicate results of data gathering. Therefore, senior support and enthusiasm is the *sine qua non* of any professional practice research project.

Setting the brief

Unless there is a clear intention, research will flounder. The brief should indicate the management objectives behind the research as well as the immediate requirements. Set out the types of questions that need to be asked and the sort of information required back.

Cost limitations should be stipulated and regular progress reports or meetings built into a timetable. Technological constraints or resources should be mentioned and sensitive areas detailed.

As with all briefs, time spent getting this right will be repaid by time saved in conducting a programme. As much background and as many guidelines as possible should be provided. It is just as relevant to set out such a brief for an internally conducted research project as it is for external researchers.

Who should do the work?

There is a tendency to think of research as a low level task, which can be relegated to secretarial level. Unless research is accorded primary importance, it will probably not lead to any useful conclusion. That is one reason why it is advisable to use external research specialists.

Exceptions are obvious. Where information can be gathered easily by using existing staff resources, it will be cheaper and easier to allocate manpower to address any finite task. Yet in most cases, research is a constantly moving vehicle, requiring experienced drivers.

The driver may be a market research organisation, briefed to conduct a complex single project or a series of activities. More ambitiously, and more controversially in view of confidentiality and caution, data capture and analysis can be farmed out – 'outsourced' – to a third party.

The advantage of either of these approaches include:

- Specialist expertise.
- Objectivity.
- Accountability.
- Knowledge of and access to existing sources of information.
- Computing and documentation systems which allow data to be processed efficiently and presented succinctly.
- Project and cost control.
- A distancing of the firm from the research process where client sensitivity might be an issue.
- Greater honesty from the client in response to questions.
- You can concentrate on running a law firm.

The problems that can arise when using external consultants are usually due to poor briefing, cultural misunderstandings, or costs running out of control. Ensure that at all times you remain ahead of the researchers, aware of what the next step will be, what the cost implications are, and what results can be expected by when.

If you are unhappy with findings or recommendations, say so. If you do not winnow out irrelevant facts, misleading interpretations or simplistic observations, someone will use the existence of such irritations to undercut the more important findings. If the research is to be accepted and used to drive new directions, it must be wholly correct when presented to decision-makers within the firm.

Presenting research

Once a project has been completed, you will rarely be in a position to say 'well, that shows us that everything is fine and nothing needs changing'. On the contrary, information gained should drive a response. Therefore, it is important to communicate results effectively within the firm, before embarking on a new course of action.

There will almost always be resistance to new data, with comfort, innate conservatism and suspicion militating against new directions. With this in mind, it is obviously important to order, clarify and control new data, so that the results of the research refute contrary or negative interpretation. Configure findings into everyday or legal language, so that meanings are immediately transparent to an audience.

Results should be presented formally to a partnership. They need to be conveyed as strategically important, not just as the pet project or hobbyhorse of an individual or clique. Often it is only through the presentation of such research that the message is absorbed – the message that the firm really is interested in the client view, not just its own.

Summary

- Determine what you want to know.
- Check that this conforms to business/marketing plans.
- Ensure that there is deep commitment to finding the information you seek. Overcome negative views.
- Gather all existing information. Establish what you can find out using internal sources.
- Set a detailed brief.
- Start from a hypothesis. Set out to prove it right, alter it, or find another hypothesis.
- Never accept a gut feeling without testing it.
- If the research can be conducted internally, accord it a high level of support and importance. If it is farmed out, make sure the objective is simple and fully understood and that clear costs are received and controlled.
- Query and contest findings until you are entirely happy with them and the methodology that uncovered them.
- Present information internally, formally, but with enthusiasm.

Hints and tips

Test any research questionnaire on a few 'guinea pigs' prior to undertaking a major project, to check that the questions are eliciting useful responses.

Consider distributing market research findings, or client satisfaction survey results, to clients. This demonstrates how seriously you view their marketplace or the importance you place on satisfying their needs.

The press in particular is obsessed by research; think how to make mileage from releasing non-confidential information to the media.

14 Direct mail

For legal and other professional firms, guidelines tend to regulate the use of direct mail. However, were they not to do so, it is likely that the majority of practitioners would be guided by their own preference and taste – which would favour limited and careful use of such a tool.

Direct mail has a poor reputation. It is associated with the mass distribution of unwanted literature – junk mail. It would be disingenuous to claim that this reputation is unmerited. Yet, along with all the existing elements in the promotional mix, direct mail can have a part to play in attracting business. Like a certain lager, it can reach the parts other initiatives cannot.

Whether we like it or not, most of us are susceptible to direct mail. Provided, of course, that one vital condition is fulfilled. That the information or offer contained in the mailing is relevant.

What is direct mail?

Any literal interpretation of the term would be misleading. Direct mail might imply a postal route from sender to recipient that missed out the agent (the post office). It could signify a straightforward or candid approach, abjuring waffle or obfuscation. Quite clearly, this is contrary to most people's experience.

In simple terms, direct mail takes a selling message or offer to a group of chosen recipients, by post. It is not requested. Mail sent out in response to an unprompted enquiry falls outside the general direct mail category.

In direct mail, any personalisation is achieved through computer mailmerging, rather than through the involvement of a personal contact.

Thus, direct mail is divorced from the personal. Used alone, or badly, it can do more harm than good to a professional firm. Yet used carefully as part of a planned strategy, it can be a valuable means of building awareness and consequent business.

A recurring theme in this book is the need to plan, so as to achieve synergy – a horrible word but an appealing concept – from a range of initiatives. Almost all PR and promotional campaigns fail to dovetail activities together. Only such integration can produce an effect where the sum is greater than its parts. And only such an effect is likely to generate a discernible increase in profile and resultant work.

Thus direct mail, as a weak solo player, must be built into a jigsaw of other activities, bounded by strategic planning. Let us take as an example the opening of a new office.

A case history

Biddleton Adams is a law firm (though it could equally be an accountancy firm or chartered surveyor). It is opening an office in Bristol. The firm believes that between 1994 and 1998 there will be a rush among residential flat owners to enfranchise, and that Bristol and Bath will provide wealthy clients and high profit margins.

Additionally, there seems to be a niche in commercial property work, where the market is showing signs of taking off.

Obviously, the firm needs to extend its local contacts in Bristol and Bath.

How can business be gained? How can a disparate, non-commercial audience be targeted?

One partner at the firm wants to put on a series of seminars. Another wants to address the local chambers of commerce. All accept that they must update their brochure, but some want to produce a bespoke property services pamphlet. One individual demands a Leasehold Reform brochure, which will address residential flat owners directly. One partner pooh-poohs 'this marketing nonsense', stating that he knows the great and the good in Bristol and Bath and can therefore meet all the right movers and shakers.

All of these are fine ideas, but they cannot solve the central dilemma. How can Biddleton Adams ascertain who might be interested in the first place?

The person responsible for pulling all these ideas together is a firm believer in using the local media. She suggests offering features to the local press (and radio stations) and running advertising in all the local papers. Copy would carry a response mechanism, whereby readers would be invited to tear off and return a section of the advertisement. All respondents would be added to the firm's mailing list (known grandiosely, if inaccurately, as its database).

In a case such as this, direct mail might be the essential ingredient in establishing a presence.

The obvious option

Law Society guidelines prevent cold calling or turning up unsolicited in someone's office. Few if any lawyers would welcome or take advantage of the opportunity to pursue either of these courses, even were they deemed acceptable. However, any firm is free to write to any individual they wish, if they feel that a service may be of potential interest.

So while lawyers need to concentrate on marketing themselves to existing clients and contacts, direct mail provides an obvious option when new clients are sought outside this circle.

What form should it take?

Direct mail can encompass anything from a letter to a pack of information. Asking for information germane to a survey, or as part of a research exercise, falls within the direct mail definition. For a law firm, most manifestations will be an invitation to meet and discuss a new service, or to attend a seminar or conference.

These lend themselves to the simplicity recommended by most direct mail experts. Classically, one asks for a yes/no response – ie gives the respondent as little difficulty as possible. Sophisticated systems allow for the 'maybe' response, but this is not recommended for anyone running a straightforward operation.

If you need to elicit more information than a simple yes or no reply, keep the material to the bare minimum. Cut wherever possible.

Consider the amount of mail you receive on your desk each morning. You are more likely to read, assimilate and respond to the succinct and helpful that the complex.

Therefore, keep copy simple. As with advertising, use a headline that grabs attention, and use text that immediately explains the benefits to the reader of responding in the way you desire. Don't get hung up on features of your product or service; major instead on how the differences will serve the client.

Replying should always be made as easy as possible. A prepaid reply card or self addressed envelope should be included with the mailing.

If you wish to undertake a direct mail exercise that requires in-depth analysis of responses, you are in the realm of market research and almost certainly need expert help.

Don't expect to gain a lot of replies to your direct mail. If 1% of a completely new list of contacts establishes contact, you are probably doing rather well.

Who to mail

The best contacts are those you know already. If you know few people or no one in a given sector, you have the option of building your own list, or buying one in.

Building a list requires combing directories, association membership lists, attendee lists from past events – and any other sources you can track down. It is laborious and probably not worth the effort.

It is preferable to use a list broker. This strange beast survives by compiling endless mailing lists on powerful databases. Contacts are categorised by job title, geographical location and a host of other codings.

If you decide you want to invite all the development directors of local authorities within a radius of 100 miles to attend an event you are holding, then someone has that information pre-prepared. Select a few brokers from directory listings, yellow pages or their own past direct mailings to you, and investigate costs and the availability of lists.

You will be able to buy the mailing details for single or multiple use, on disk, label or as a list. If you are buying for single use only, the cost will be less. Do not think you can then reuse the list; it will include an address where, if a subsequent mailing is received, horns will go off, whistles will be blown and you will be charged with various heinous offences.

Summary

- Use direct mail as part of a campaign or to support a primary activity.
- Don't direct mail your new brochure to your client, unless it is ancillary to an invitation, an announcement, or similar.
- Keep both copy and design simple.
- Build in a response mechanism.
- If you ask for a reply, make it easy to do so.
- Ensure that there is a reason to reply – ie a benefit in so doing.
- Set your sights low. Unless you are contacting people you know, response levels may be well under 5%.
- Buy in lists from brokers rather than compile your own – unless you have an authoritative source which has been 'cleaned' – ie checked and updated, recently.

Hints and tips

- Avoid Friday mailings. You do not want to be part of the Monday morning pile of mail that gets junked because the reader has no time to consider anything not seen as essential.
- Put yourself in the shoes of the intended recipient. If you feel uncomfortable, don't mail.
- When buying a list from a broker, arrange to pay for multiple use if you know that there will be future mailings. This should reduce the per mailing cost significantly.

15 Continuous promotion

Promoting a law firm is not a stand-alone feature. One can make time to perform a specific task – plan a seminar or perhaps write an article. Yet in addition to such undertakings, everything you do has a promotional aspect.

Every letter or document produced reflects more than the expertise contained. Every meeting does more than update clients or make progress. Every encounter represents more than discussion or negotiation.

Common to all the above is the indistinct concept of creating an impression. As aware as most of us are that we create, alter or perpetuate an impression during every encounter or transaction, we understand very little about it. Not knowing exactly how the process works, or how we can direct it, we tend to leave it to take care of itself.

On the personal level, and at its worst, this translates into: 'This is how I am. Take it or leave it.'

If such a let-alone attitude is true in terms of creating a personal impression, it is doubly so when it comes to promoting an organisation. Here we see the blinkered approach: 'This is the firm. Buy us. We're good.'

While no one in their right mind would utter either of the above statements to a client or contact, such unstated beliefs can underlie an apathetic ignorance of day to day promotion.

Fortunately, this is rare. Most lawyers take particular pains over the routine aspects of promoting a practice – letter writing, document production and so forth.

One reason is that they have spent years doing just this. The main reason, however, is that there is an obvious and immediate rationale. Such pains are taken to build existing client relationships. They serve to develop the practice of the individual, not the more amorphous indirect interests of the firm.

Thus, the layout of a letter may become of vital importance to the average solicitor. Getting the margins just so, indenting and numbering correctly, using italics appropriately – all assume great prominence in the production of the finished opus.

Things tend to go wrong in two main respects. One is conflict between any established norm within the firm, and the specific preferences of the individual, in terms of this layout. The other is in the content of the letter.

Establishing a norm

Several times in this book, and many times outside it, the point has been made that it is important to achieve consistency of appearance in a firm's promotional materials. Contrary to the jaundiced opinion of the 'can't change, won't change' minority, this view does not represent a fraud perpetrated on the legal profession by corporate identity consultants.

If a client receives several letters from different people within a firm, each reflecting a different style, there may or may not be a conscious reaction. However, impressions are not made consciously. They are absorbed. And in this case, they will not be favourable. The impression will be one of unconnected diversity, when every firm needs to show that its diverse talents are harnessed together. The letters speak of a lack of central control, injurious to the health of the firm-client relationship.

The lesson arising from such observations is obvious. The preferences of the few must give way to the norm. This means, of course, that time and effort, those two rare commodities, must be found to ensure that the standard approach looks good, is easy to use and clear to read. Once such a template has been established, no one should be allowed to diverge from it.

This guidance should take the form of illustrated examples, where possible, with written instructions kept to the minimum. People will simply ignore tomes of detail.

Content

Poor content provides the second, more contentious, aspect of letters and documentation. This has nothing to do with technical skills. The author of these words is probably outranked on the IQ, qualifications and grammatical knowledge scale by most lawyers. It goes back to the core of communication, where the difference between good and bad is simply the ability to provide information in a form that is comprehensible and of interest to the listener/reader.

210

For centuries, lawyers have been taught to be lawyers in such a way that they are educated away from becoming communicators. The factual absoluteness of legislation leads to an approach where lawyers tend to make statements rather than consider the first rule of communication: think from the recipient's point of view first, your own second.

Legal language and concepts are so complicated that it takes an enormous effort to translate back into English. The bedevilling fear that simplification will lead to inaccuracy means that few people follow successfully the course which leads to getting both the law and its communication equally right.

A simple approach is to divorce the two. Leave the law to the legal documentation and the communicating to the most appropriate form, whether this be a covering letter or a meeting. As with a seminar, this letter or meeting is designed to convey only the essence of the law, but has as its ancillary and often main objective the promotion of you as expert and the firm as fount of all knowledge.

If you are writing a covering letter, keep it concise. Tell the client what it accompanies and make sure that any notable achievements in conducting the work are at least hinted at.

Groucho Marx once received a letter from his bank manager ending in the usual bromide: 'If I can be of service to you, please do not hesitate to call me.'

Marx responded: 'Dear Sir, Please steal some money from the account of your richest client and credit it to me.'

Few of us would have the wit to reply in such vein, but few of us lack the wit to note and even be offended by such lazy clichés. Keep them from your letters.

Tell your readers what they want to know – not in the sense of covering up bad news, of course, but in delivering yourself of pithy, punchy and valuable information. Cut out the waffle. Go back over a draft letter and excise anything that is not essential. Dictating is a wonderful process, but you can wreck a good letter by relying on a first run alone.

Enthusiasm

Enthusiasm without knowledge is charming but unlikely to earn respect. Knowledge without enthusiasm is far preferable, but is dry and demotivating. Yet ally a firm grasp of pertinent facts to an enthusiastic delivery and you have a potent communication tool. An exponent of such an art is an invaluable promoter of the firm's and his or her own abilities.

Enthusiasm can set a letter alight, infect a meeting and win over doubters. It is unusual in the legal world, where undue reverence mixes with due respect. Being unusual, it is all the more valuable and valued when it makes an appearance. Clients tend to live in a non-legal world, where enthusiasm is less frowned upon.

However, a note of (probably unnecessary) caution. In Glengarry Glen Ross, David Mamet's had noted salesmen operated under the slogan 'ABC' – 'Always Be Closing'. In legal markets, enthusiasm is fine, while the ABC approach is not. David Mosey suggests that lawyers contemplating any marketing initiative 'might try the less catchy acronym 'DBTP' – 'Don't be too pushy'.

Social promotion

Such a note of caution might apply when promoting a firm continues outside working hours. A dinner party is as much a forum as an association lunch, and many useful contacts are made at cocktail parties and other social gatherings. Always have a stock of business cards in your wallet or purse.

Much fun can be had devising games and stratagems for making the most of social opportunities to promote a firm. Indeed, there are those who make a living from such pursuits. Frankly, many of these are likely to appear crass, obvious and inappropriate. Far more important is the ability to convey enthusiasm, and to differentiate.

All law firms are the same in essence. Specialisations subdivide firms into separate categories, but there is usually someone else doing exactly what you do. If this is not the case, you need only convey the fact that you can provide a needed service to whoever seems in need. In the majority of cases, you need to explain what is different about your firm. Succinctly.

If a social event throws up a potentially interested client or contact, you need to be in a position to rattle off two or three impressive features of your firm, translating these instantly into the benefits people such as your new friend tend to experience and come to expect. Leave the 'social bonding' – or, to be more British, the 'getting to know each other' – to take care of itself. Concentrate instead on putting across your enthusiastic belief in your firm. If you have a well rehearsed means of doing this, you will be a perfect ambassador for the practice.

Research yourself

This raises an embarrassing observation. Many people do not know what their firms do. Extraordinary as it seems, there are large firms whose partners do not know each other, medium sized practices where services provided are a mystery to fee earners, and smaller firms who have no idea of individuals' more specialised areas of expertise.

This is where the importance of internal communication can prove vital. People have walked away from millions of pounds of work, simply through ignorance of their own (firm's) potential.

Therefore it is vital that internal records are kept and circulated, showing who has developed expertise in which fields. Consideration should be given to whether work in progress should be reported beyond the partnership, through internal newsletter reports or regular updates.

Often, the corporate brochure rewrite reveals aspects of a practice which surprises the partnership. With this being the case, it is clearly important that, at the very least, people read and are conversant with the firm's brochure.

The result of successfully circulated internal information is effortless persuasion at a social or business encounter that the firm has the breadth of knowledge, the appropriate specialists and the weight of experience equal to the task contemplated by the new contact.

What follows depends on circumstance. In a semi-social situation (ie corporate hospitality or an association event) it is a good idea to annotate the reverse of business cards, noting immediately the essence of facts learned and actions to be taken. Keep your own business cards in one pocket and new ones in the other. Make sure that, if you have promised to put x in touch with y, you harry x until he or she has made that contact.

Associations

Too many firms join too many associations and never exploit the opportunities. The golden rule is to allocate one or two people to every industry forum and make them responsible for attending on a regular basis. Sending a different person to each meeting is largely a waste of time.

The partner or fee earner representing the firm through a professional body should be expected to seek, conduct and report on initiatives taken. Usually, mileage only follows time spent building personal contacts. Consequently, a long view has to be taken, leading to regular reviews.

Keeping in touch

Whether it be with ex-clients, fellow cocktail party guests, co-delegates to a conference or any other irregular contact, make a point of staying in touch. If you see a newspaper clipping that might be of interest, send it. Make a point of contacting key people at least once a quarter, if for no other reason than to be seen being interested. If you do not indicate as much, there is no reason to be considered should work be in the offing.

Summary

- Think about the appearance given, and the impression received, through every form of contact you have with a client.
- Aim for consistency of letter layout. Set templates. Keep instructions simple and visual (rather than conveyed through complex verbiage).
- Keep letters law-free and jargon-free. Leave the law to legal documentation.
- Keep letters concise and communicative. A letter should explain legal facts in layman's terms, add value, ask for information or provide a context. It should not contain platitudes or waffle.
- If a letter summarises a document, it should only do so if this will help the recipient read the document; if it prevents him or her from doing so, it may prove counterproductive.
- Convey enthusiasm. This will be unexpected and seen as appealing and complimentary.
- Plan how best to convey the strengths and uniqueness of the firm when asked about it in an informal context. A speech will be off-putting, but so is an uncertain response. Practice a sentence or two that would impress you, if you were a client in search of a firm like yours.
- Get to know your own firm. If you don't know what is done in a department, find out.
- Read your own literature. It is often the best way to gain the knowledge required to promote the breadth of your service.
- Join associations to attend them, not simply to rid yourself of unwanted money.
- Keep in touch with useful contacts. Manufacture reasons to call them. If you have not spoken within a fixed period of time, engineer an encounter.

Hints and tips

- Don't wait to be instructed: if you can see a logical course of action, suggest it to the client.
- Always be on the look out for new directions from a client. If they mention a course of action, send them appropriate promotional literature from the firm to be kept on file in case matters develop.

- Introduce anecdotes that demonstrate the firm's experience and track record, when business conversation veers in that direction.
- If you meet a useful contact, make sure details are added to the firm's database.

Appendix I

Solicitors' Publicity Code 1990 (with consolidated amendments to 1 January 1992)

The Code is contained in *The Guide to the Professional Conduct of Solicitors 1993*. This is available from the Law Society. Space and relevance does not permit wholesale reproduction of the rules. The following observations and excerpts, however, have been selected because they either cover contentious ground, or because they deal with issues which are likely to arise in the day to day conduct of promotional initiatives.

Conservative – but liberalising

The Code today is far less restrictive than at its inception. Its earliest attempts to police the dignity and gravitas of the profession led to something of a straitjacket being imposed. The 1990 relaxations, and subsequent amendments, have allowed sensible freedoms without threatening an explosion of crass behaviour.

Some aspects remain vague. For example, bad taste publicity (naturally) is prohibited, but is defined only as taking any form that 'might reasonably be regarded as being' in bad taste. No publicity shall 'be inaccurate or misleading in any way' is a worthy observation, but lapses might be rather difficult to pin down absolutely.

Specialisation

However, a laudable alteration is the freedom to claim expertise without having to be a member of an appropriate panel. Paragraph 2(b) reads, 'It is not improper for a claim to be made that a solicitor (or a registered foreign lawyer) is a specialist, or an expert, in a particular field provided that such a claim can be justified.'

217

While looseness comes into play once again, justification being highly subjective, this change has allowed genuine specialists to promote themselves as such.

Comparison

No publicity may make direct comparison or criticism with any other identifiable solicitor. The exceptions would be general statements, or the using of any objective, bona fide research survey conducted by a third party.

Cold calling

No unsolicited phone calls or visits can be made for publicity purposes, unless to a former/existing client or professional connection, or to another solicitor. An exception is made when publicising a specific commercial property or properties.

There is no stipulation against writing to potential clients or contacts. Indeed, the Commentary to the Solicitors' Publicity Code 1990 given in *The Guide to the Professional Conduct of Solicitors 1993* (point 6, p 217) states that, 'Unsolicited mailshots may be sent and can be targeted.'

Naming clients

Another recent change allows firms to name clients, provided that 'the client gives consent which, in the case of advertisements and directories, shall be in writing'.

Note that the naming of clients when presenting at Beauty Parades, is covered by the Professional Standards Bulletin No 10, as published in *The Gazette* of 17 December 1993. This is governed under the basic principles of confidentiality, rather than advertising. Thus, the client may only be named if both the work conducted and the fact that the firm represents the client are both matters of public knowledge. The nature of the work conducted on the client's behalf must, of course, remain confidential.

Section 6 of the Code has caused some problems of interpretation. It allows firms to use designations other than 'solicitor', provided that the word 'solicitor/s' is also used. A description need not contain the word 'solicitor' – but any form of designation must do so.

218

The easiest course of action on the face of this distinction must surely be to ensure that 'solicitor/s' appear as a matter of course on letterheads, brass plates, advertisements etc.

Outside England and Wales, 'lawyer/s' is acceptable, provided that these so described are appropriately qualified (the 1977 Lawyers Services Directive provides the definition).

Passing off

Firms should be careful to ensure that any member of staff named in publicity who does not hold a practicing certificate has his or her role defined unambiguously. Also, paragraph 7(a)(iii) warns that 'Practitioners are reminded of the danger of inadvertently holding out persons as partners in a firm by inclusion of both partners' and non-partners' names in a list. The status of non-partners must be indicated for avoidance of doubt whenever a situation of inadvertent holding out might otherwise arise.'

The terms 'associate', 'assistant' and 'consultant' should be used with care. Each must only be used to indicate a solicitor holding a current practising certificate.

Getting it wrong

Any breaches of the Code, provided they are not deemed heinous, should result only in a slap on the wrist. As the Rules state (Note to paragraph 17), 'Where contravention of this code is not serious, the Council encourages local law societies to bring breaches to the attention of the solicitors concerned. Serious or persistent cases should be reported to the Solicitors Complaints Bureau.'

Appendix II

Selected Bibliography

Professional Services Marketing, Neil Morgan, Butterworth Heinemann, 1991.

Marketing for Lawyers, Matthew Moore, Law Society, 1990.

Selling Professional Services, Bernard Katz, Gower, 1988.

Marketing Legal Services, Ed SC Silkin QC, Waterlow, 1984.

Marketing and Communication Techniques for Architects, LC Ryness, Longman, 1992.

Effective Speaking, Christina Stuart, Pan, 1988.

Making Major Sales, Neil Rackham, Gower, 1994.

Public Relations Techniques, Frank Jefkins, Heinemann, 1989.

The Craft of Copywriting, Alastair Crompton, Hutchinson, 1990.

The Public Relations Casebook, Capper & Cunard, Kogan Page, 1990.

Appendix III

A selection of addresses and contacts

The Law Society, 50 Chancery Lane, London, WC2A 1SX. Telephone 071 242 1222.

Professional Services Marketing Group, Po Box 353, Uxbridge, UB10 0UN. Telephone 0895 256972.

Informal Legal Marketing Forum, c/o Linda Phelan, Director of Marketing, DJ Freeman, 43 Fetter Lane, London, EC4A 1NA. Telephone 071 583 4055.

The Chartered Institute of Marketing, Moor Hall, Cookham, Maidenhead, Berkshire, SL6 9QH. Telephone 06285 24922.

The Institute of Public Relations, The Old Trading House, 15 Northburgh Street, London, EC1V 0PR. Telephone 071 253 5151.

The Public Relations Consultants Association, Willow House, Willow Place, Victoria, London, SW1P 1JH. Telephone 071 233 6026.

The CAM Foundation, Abford House, 15 Wilton Road, London, SW1V 1NJ. Telephone 071 828 7506 (Training Courses).

The Sports Council, 16 Upper Woburn Place, London, WC1H 0QP. Telephone 071 388 1277.

Romeike & Curtis, Hale House, 290-296 Green Lanes, London, N13 5TP. Telephone 081 882 0155 (Press Cutting Service).

Two Ten Communications Ltd, 210 Old Street, London, EC1V 9UN. Telephone 071 490 8111 (Media Directories).

The Press Association, 85 Fleet Street, London, EC4P 4BE. Telephone 071 353 7440.

SpeakEasy Training Ltd, Premier House, 309 Ballards Lane, London N12 8NE. Telephone 081 446 0797 (Presentation Training).